HARDBALL

HARDBALL

Are You Playing to Play or Playing to Win?

George Stalk
Robert Lachenauer

with John Butman

HARVARD BUSINESS SCHOOL PRESS
BOSTON, MASSACHUSETTS

Library of Congress Cataloging-in-Publication Data
Stalk, George, 1951–
    Hardball : are you playing to play or playing to win? / George Stalk, Rob Lachenauer, with John Butman.
        p. cm.
    Includes bibliographical references and index.
    ISBN 1-59139-167-9
    1. Success in business. 2. Competition. 3. Strategic planning. 4. Industrial management. 5. Toughness (Personality trait). I. Lachenauer, Rob. II. Butman, John. III. Title.
    HF5386.S776 2004
    658.4'012—dc22

                                                                    2004008850

The paper used in this publication meets the requirements of the American National Standard for Permanence of Paper for Publications and Documents in Libraries and Archives Z39.48–1992.

CONTENTS

HARDBALL

The Hardball Manifesto

The winners in business have always played hardball. When companies play hardball it means they use every legitimate resource and strategy available to them to gain advantage over their competitors. When they achieve competitive advantage they attract more customers, gain market share, boost profits, reward their employees, and weaken their competitors' positions. They then reinvest their gains in their businesses to improve product quality, expand their offerings, and improve their processes, to further strengthen their competitive advantage. When they can continue this virtuous cycle of activity for a prolonged period, they can transform their competitive advantage into a position even more powerful and desirable—they can achieve decisive advantage. With that, they put themselves into a far more powerful and influential position than that of just the market leader. They can use their decisive advantage to bring about fundamental change to an entire industry, put their competitors into a reactive position, cause their partners and suppliers to make adjustments, and deliver so much value to their customers that their market share grows larger still.

This kind of winning through competitive advantage may sound like nothing more than good, serious, and sensible business practice. But hardball companies are further distinguished by their attitude and behavior. They play with such a total commitment to the game, such a fierceness of execution, and such a relentless drive to maximize their strengths that they look very different from other companies that have admirable performance and sound business skills. Hardball players always play to win, in every aspect of the game. They always seek decisive victory. They don't want to win a 2–1 squeaker. They would prefer a 9–2 rout.

Softball players have no competitive advantage or, if they have one, may not know what it is or may be unable to exploit it. Some softballers can drift along for years, finding ways—through trade loading, for example, or cost cutting—to stay afloat from quarter to quarter. A few may seek to disguise their poor performance through activities—such as creating shell customers—that are questionable, if not illegal. In the parlance of pitching, such companies are throwing junk.

We believe that in our society it is the fundamental purpose of companies to compete as hard as they can against one another. In the September 13, 1970, edition of the *New York Times Magazine* Nobel laureate Milton Friedman quoted from his book *Capitalism and Freedom* when he wrote, "There is one and only one social responsibility of business—to use its resources and engage in activities designed to increase its profits so long as it stays within the rules of the game, which is to say, engages in open and free competition without deception or fraud."

Friedman's comments sparked a debate about corporate purpose that raged in corporate suites across the country and around the world, in the halls of academe, and in the influential "chat societies" of our nation's capital. The debate continues to this day.

Bruce Henderson, founder of The Boston Consulting Group, fundamentally agreed with Friedman, but placed even more emphasis on the importance of competition. In 1973, troubled by the actions taken against IBM and AT&T in the name of competitive "fairness," Henderson wrote: "The leading competitor in every business should increase his market share steadily. Failure to do so is prima facie evidence of failure to compete."

Henderson went on to describe the virtuous cycle that creates decisive advantage. "Competitors' market shares should be unstable. Low cost competitors should displace higher cost competitors. Customers should share the benefits of lower cost through lower price with those suppliers who make it possible. Any failure to gain market share even with lower cost is self-evident restraint of trade. . . ."

Henderson concluded by saying that companies that did not operate in this way would lead to a failure of their industry to "concentrate" (consolidate and improve), which would lead to an even larger failure— "a failure of the national economy to optimize productivity and reduce inflation." In other words, as self-centered as playing hardball and seeking to win may appear, it is, in fact, essential to the health and strength of the larger economy and our society.[1]

This book follows in the tradition of Milton Friedman, Bruce Henderson, and many others who believe that it is the function of companies to compete as hard as they can to gain customers and profits, with the goal of achieving the greatest advantage they can over their competitors.

From our experience in working with clients over many years, in many industries, and many countries throughout the world, we know that the leaders of the world's most successful companies—the hardball winners—believe it is their obligation to their shareholders, customers, employees, and society to seek and exploit their competitive advantage to the fullest. And, when possible, the hardball leaders will push that advantage to the point where competitors are squeezed and even feel pain. When the competitors find themselves in this position, they have two choices. They can play softball, which means using non-strategic means to get society to bend its rules to hobble the success of their hardball opponents. Or, they can seek out the chinks in the armor of hardball players to change the rules of the game to their favor. We advocate the second. Business, like life, goes on as a never-ending cycle of achieving advantage, facing threats from bold and innovative competitors, and adjusting to or succumbing to these challenges.

But, when an organization achieves advantage, it develops a tendency to continue operating with the same strategy or model that produced the advantage. It is the leader's main role, then, to keep alive the quest for advantage. As Roger Enrico, former chairman of PepsiCo, said to us, it's impossible for an organization to "shadowbox" its way to continued advantage building. It is the task of the leader to make his people understand that their company's advantage is always in peril and, if necessary, to create an opponent against whom the organization can focus its efforts.

In addition to strong leaders, hardball competitors also have what is generally called "good management." In the development of this book, and in the writing of the *Harvard Business Review* article that preceded it, however, we have been criticized for downplaying the importance of the "soft" issues, such as culture and employee relations. We do not mean to downplay them, but rather to put them in the context of strategy. Good management is a necessary but not sufficient condition of business success. Differences in profitability correlate very strongly with differences in competitive advantage. We believe that a management team that can provide a hardball strategy and push the organization to use it to gain competitive advantage is the most likely to deliver benefit—emotional, intellectual, social, financial, and professional—to its people. By championing hardball, we are not advocating that we discard or ignore all we have learned about how to create good relationships with people both inside and outside the organization. On the contrary, we believe that people who work for and with hardball players are exceptionally well rewarded and among the most fulfilled people you will find in business.

THE CHARACTERISTICS OF THE HARDBALL PLAYER

Above all, hardball players play to win. They employ strategies that will gain them competitive advantage, which in turn will bring them substantial sales margins, above-average profit margins and earnings, lower-than-average debt, higher-than-average credit ratings, and most important, leading market share.

Dell is a hardball player. Its competitive advantage is its cost structure. When Hewlett-Packard announced weak results because of price competition in PCs, Dell announced an across-the-board price cut—delivering a swift kick to its rival when it was down. No other PC maker approaches Dell's market share or profitability.

Hardball players don't settle for competitive advantage, however. As they build revenues, profits, and market share, they also relentlessly cut costs, improve systems, and introduce new products and services to draw new customers in. Their goal is to strengthen their competitive advantage until it becomes so decisive they are able to set the agenda and pace of innovation in their industry. But because they continue to feed the virtuous cycle, they never sit on their lead and usually enjoy a much-longer-than-average lifespan.

Toyota is a hardball player. Its competitive advantage is a production system that enables the company to manufacture, with unsurpassed productivity, cars of unequalled quality. Using it, Toyota has relentlessly attacked the Big Three automakers where their will to defend was the weakest, beginning in the 1980s with compact cars, then with mid- and full-size cars, and now, in a coup de grâce, with trucks and SUVs, Detroit's final remaining profit centers. Toyota's production system is no secret, and other manufacturers have tried to copy it. So far, no company has been able to use it to threaten Toyota's leadership.

Sometimes hardball players have to play a little rough and, when they do, they don't apologize for it. But they never jeopardize their customers, don't make moves that weaken the industry or benefit only themselves, and, of course, they never do anything illegal.

Wal-Mart created competitive advantage with a superior logistics system that enables it to cut costs and build volume. The company demands that its suppliers work with it to reduce costs throughout the supply chain. When Rubbermaid could not, or would not, rationalize its delivery system to consolidate shipments from different factories, Wal-Mart took simplification into its own hands. It drastically reduced the number of Rubbermaid items it would stock, a hardball move that significantly affected Rubbermaid's total sales volume.

Hardball players create competitive advantage and build it into decisive advantage by keeping their focus on the heart of the matter—a very small set of vital issues whose resolution will determine the future of the organization. Hardball leaders get their people to deal with the heart of the matter and do not allow them to get distracted from it.

The president of Wausau Papers, for example, believed his lackluster Brokaw division could build competitive advantage by dramatically improving customer service, especially on low-volume specialty orders. For years, the company had focused on cost-cutting, limiting product variety, and never sending out a delivery truck until it was filled with orders. The president forced his people to focus on a new set of issues that drove superior service: efficient order taking, quick machine set-up and process control, fast packaging, and availability of trucks. When the head of logistics couldn't get inside the heart of the matter, the president made a hardball move and replaced him.

Not only does hardball create success for the player, it benefits the economy, as Milton Friedman and Bruce Henderson both argued. It is efficient. It cleanses the market. It makes all companies stronger and more vital. It results in product and service innovation, and more affordable products and services, and it creates more satisfied customers.

But the practices of hardball players often raise eyebrows and provoke critical attention. "Can Anything Stop Toyota?" asked a headline in *BusinessWeek.* "Is Wal-Mart Good for America?" worried the *New York Times.* "Dell: Meanest Kid on the Block" was the take in *Fortune.* Something seems not quite kosher, and certainly not very nice, about the way hardball players go about winning.[2]

Much of this public criticism comes about as a reaction to the reprehensible, and often illegal, behavior of the genuinely bad boys of business who have been exposed, deposed, and even incarcerated in the past decade. These people are not hardball players. They are softballers, whose companies pretended to create competitive advantage and high profitability. But it was an imaginary advantage that now appears to have been based on accounting games and house-of-cards acquisition activity.

The negative view of hardball players is further reinforced by the current state of management discipline, at least as it is expressed in the press, popular management literature, and the curricula of many business schools. For years, the business world has been focusing on that constellation of issues that are generally called "soft," including customer care, employee empowerment, talent management, corporate culture, and corporate governance. These are extremely important issues, but the problem has been that they have generally been considered as stand-alone activities, almost as if they are strategies unto themselves. But without a business strategy that will create or strengthen competitive advantage, no amount of customer care or employee motivation will bring a company success or longevity.

Hardball companies pay plenty of attention to the soft issues—of reward and recognition, culture, customer relations, and leadership—but they approach them within the context of their business strategy. Their people feel good about their companies because they know they are playing to win, and businesspeople love winning. Hardball companies have vitality because they go to the heart of the matter, and people love to feel that what they are doing is true and that it is important. Hardball companies attract and retain talented people because they are strong enough to compensate their employees well and assure them of a bright future.

Even so, the word *hardball* may be difficult for some people to swallow. Some of our colleagues and peer reviewers were concerned that readers would get the wrong idea, and assume that we were writing in praise of heartless robber barons, ruthless corporate raiders, and executives consumed with greed. Quite the opposite.

Hardball is not about extreme executive behavior, playing outside the lines of legality, or even about being mean. It is about creating discomfort for others and tolerating it yourself. In baseball, a hardball move is when a pitcher faces an aggressive batter and sends him a message by throwing a 98-mile-an-hour pitch high and inside. The pitcher does not intend to hit the batter and he has sufficient skill and control not to. That is a tough, perfectly legal, and very effective hardball move.

Some of the negative reaction to hardball players comes from the softball players, the ones who don't have the resources, skill, or will to compete against hardballers. Rather than find a way to attack the major player, or find a new source of competitive advantage for themselves, softball players resort to softball tactics. In baseball, softball players kick dirt at the umpire, spit toward their opponent's dugout, or get their base runner to show his spikes as he slides into second base. Softball companies lobby for trade restrictions and seek market regulations that will hobble the leader. They will make half-hearted copies of their competitor's products. They will seed negative stories about their competitors in the press or harass them with groundless complaints in the courts. But these tactics (they're not strategies) rarely change the game or bring competitive advantage to the companies that employ them. As they posture and pout, the softball players let billions of dollars of shareholder value drip, drip, drip into oblivion.

In the next ten years, companies are going to move more quickly, act smarter, and battle more fiercely than ever before. There will be the leading players and lots of niche players, but very few, if any, players in between. The softball players that have survived until now (many airlines, certain automakers, plenty of health-care providers) don't have long to live.

Only the hardball players will survive. Only the hardball players should survive.

THE PRINCIPLES OF HARDBALL

Hardball players live by five principles:

They focus relentlessly on competitive advantage. The history of business is littered with the remains of companies whose competitive advantage, once robust, has withered away. Hardball players strive to continually widen the performance gap between themselves and competitors. They are not satisfied with today's competitive advantage—they want tomorrow's.

Hardball players believe in empirically proven advantage. They know what their advantage is and exploit it relentlessly. They don't deceive themselves or cheat. They measure their competitive advantage and differentiate theirs from their competitors. Softball players talk about competitive advantage, but few of them are able to put a finger on exactly what theirs is or quantify it.

Hardball companies relentlessly pursue competitive advantage and create a virtuous circle that continually strengthens it. Wal-Mart began playing hardball by creating a distribution system that reduced transportation costs, increased inventory turns, and gave it a competitive advantage. Then it went to "every day low prices" to stabilize demand, further reduce costs, and build volume. Next they leveraged their huge sales volume to gain influence over shipments from suppliers and to dictate merchandising and product mix, reducing prices further and adding yet more volume. Wal-Mart continues to tighten the bolts on this system, with no signs of shearing.

They strive to convert competitive advantage into decisive advantage. Unlike plain old competitive advantage, which can be fleeting, decisive advantage puts you out of the reach of your competitors. Decisive advantage is systemically reinforcing. The better you get at it, the harder it is for competitors to compete against it or take it away. For example, as you get bigger than your competitors, your costs go down further, enabling you to further increase your market share. The hardball competitor may have created an economic system that is unassailable. Or established a relationship with a customer or a supplier that is not available to its competitors. Or developed capabilities, such as fast product development or superior customer knowledge, that cannot be replicated.

Toyota's decisive advantage—which is built on its superior production system—has enabled Toyota to grow its global market share from 5 percent in 1980 to 11 percent today, with each point of market share worth about $10 billion in revenue. Toyota's market capitalization in 2003 is greater than that of GM and Ford combined. The company says their goal for global market share is 15 percent by 2010. Does anyone want to bet they will not achieve it?

They employ the indirect attack. Hardball players often avoid direct confrontation with competitors. This may seem counterintuitive—you might assume the hardball player would take an aggressive in-your-face approach—but military history shows that most decisive victories have been won through indirect attack. "The indirect attack is by far the most hopeful and economic form of strategy," writes B. H. Liddell Hart, a military historian. "The most consistently successful commanders when faced by an enemy in a position that was strong naturally or materially have hardly ever attacked it in a direct way."[3]

Southwest Airlines (SWA) launched a classic indirect attack. They chose not to compete head-to-head with the major airlines at the biggest city hubs where the majors were strongest. Rather, Southwest built up operations in secondary airports. In the Washington, D.C., metropolitan region, for example, Southwest started operations from the Baltimore-Washington airport—the third largest airport in the region—with twelve flights a day. Now they have 163 departures from BWI.

Once Southwest was established and had built its customer base in the smaller airports, the major carriers faced a dilemma. Should they try to compete directly with Southwest in the smaller airports where they had no competitive advantage? If they did, and were successful, they would probably end up stealing business from their own big hub operations. Or should they create new airlines to compete with Southwest? No major carrier has yet found a successful answer.

They exploit their employees' will to win. More than smarts are required to play hardball. As Jimmy Doolittle, the Air Force colonel who flew a celebrated raid in World War II, put it: "Victory belongs to those who believe in it the most." (Or, at least, that's how Alec Baldwin, who played Doolittle in the movie *Pearl Harbor,* put it.)

When Bill Irwin sought to create growth for Batesville Casket Company, he faced resistance from his central office management team, manufacturing staff, distribution center managers, and materials suppliers. To get his management team focused on the importance of quality, he placed a casket riddled with manufacturing defects in the executive suite where they could not avoid seeing it every day. To get his manufacturing people on board, he spent hours in the factory talking up the strategy, explaining the importance of the new production processes. To get the best performance from his suppliers, he promised speedy payment if they would come in-house and manage their inventories from the factory floor. He was tough and demanding, a no-nonsense hardball player. But he wanted his company to win, his people responded, and Batesville built decisive advantage in the burial casket industry.

To achieve competitive advantage, people must be action-oriented, always impatient with the status quo. Fortunately, the will to win can be fostered; softball players can be transformed into hardball players. But as your competitive advantage grows, it gets harder to exploit your employees' will to win. "The number-one threat is us," Herb Kelleher, the former CEO of Southwest Airlines, told his people at a big company meeting. "We must not let success breed complacency, cockiness, greediness, laziness, indifference, preoccupation with nonessentials; bureaucracy; hierarchy; quarrelsomeness; or obliviousness to threats posed by the outside world."[4]

They draw a bright line in the caution zone. To play hardball means being aware of when you are entering the "caution zone"—that area, so rich in possibility, that lies between the place where society clearly says you can play the game of business and the place where society clearly says you can't. Before you enter the caution zone, you have to know where the unacceptable area is and draw a bright line for your company that marks the edge, the limit beyond which you will not venture. It is the leader's responsibility to draw the line and make it very bright and clear. You can't expect your employees to operate in the caution zone without clear guidance from you. So hardball players do their homework. They know their industries cold. They get legal and accounting counsel to help them determine what they can do and what they can't. Their leadership knows where the bright line is, lets everybody know when they're getting close to it, and takes corrective action as soon as anybody steps over it.

The edge of the caution zone is sometimes hard to determine. Sometimes the leader draws the bright line in the wrong place. Sometimes the organization misunderstands where it is. Some say that Microsoft operates so deep in the caution zone that it often steps over the bright line. By disregarding the damage it can inflict on competitors by refusing to share ownership of the PC desktop, for example, Microsoft found itself in a legal morass. But, by arguing that its customers benefit from the approach, it moved itself back from the edge, which undoubtedly reduced the impact of the numerous legal attacks by competitors and regulators.

When hardball players operate in the caution zone, they must take extra care. Although the bright line that separates legal activity from illegal activity is relatively easy to see (but not always) the boundary between what is morally and socially acceptable business practice from what is intolerable and shameful is harder to define. Society accepts certain competitive behaviors as part of the game, and to employ them entails little risk. The "fake," or feint, for example, is a standard hardball move in all team sports and in business. The high-technology industry has employed the fake—known as vaporware—for years. In the auto industry, phony prototypes are taken out for test runs or photos leaked to the press to mislead competitors. Fakes are an accepted part of business life, and good fakers are to be admired.

There are many practices that are illegal or that lie right along the boundary of illegality, including such anticompetitive practices and nasty behaviors as kickbacks, bribes, smears, and threats. Hardball players never engage in such activities. If anyone inside their organization does, they take action against them. That's why Gillette, a company working to regain its hardball mindset, blew the whistle on one of its merchandising managers for taking kickbacks from vendors. He eventually was sentenced to more than three years in jail.

There are a few questions to ask yourself that can make it easier to recognize the caution zone and establish a bright line at its outer boundary:

- *Will the proposed action break any laws?* If it will, don't do it. (Duh.) Hardball is not about accounting shenanigans, contract manipulation, snatching of trade secrets, or predatory pricing.

- *Is the proposed action good for the customer?* If it is, even an action that might be legally challenged could be found to be acceptable by the courts or legislators. If it isn't good for consumers, however, you may create an army of protestors eager to assist in your downfall. Hardball players never gain competitive advantage by manipulating or weakening their customers.

- *Will competitors be directly hurt by an action?* Putting competitors in situations in which they inflict damage on themselves is acceptable, such as enticing a rival to invest in an area where it has no hope of winning. Overtly hurting a competitor by buying a key supplier and then cutting off your rival, even if the move is legal, may win you the wrath of others you do business with.

- *Will an action hit a nerve with a special interest group in a way that might damage the company?* There are many organizations that want to express their social or political views through protest action. The opponents of sports utility vehicles, for example, vandalized car dealerships. The opponents of animal testing burst into Gillette product launches wearing bunny suits. Such activities can create public relations disasters, hurt sales, and damage a brand.

- *Will the action provoke positive change?* Sometimes it makes sense to deliberately take on a special interest group, regulatory body, or other organization in order to improve business conditions or change the status quo in such a way that substantially benefits customers. Ryanair pushed up against industry restrictions to catalyze airline deregulation in Europe. Now consumers can fly between European cities for as little as a tenth of what it cost before deregulation. Walter Wriston, as Chairman of Citibank (now Citi), challenged banking regulations that limited the ability of depositors to earn interest on certain types of accounts. Such hardball players, driven by a cause they believe to be beneficial to themselves and to society, can reposition the bright line.

THE HARDBALL STRATEGIES

There are many strategies in the hardball playbook; indeed, any strategy that provides a competitive advantage is a hardball move. There are, however, a handful of classic hardball strategies that have proved, over the decades, to be particularly effective in generating competitive advantage, and they are the ones we describe in this book:

Unleash massive and overwhelming force. Although hardball players prefer the indirect attack, they sometimes surprise and overcome their competitors with a frontal assault. Massive and overwhelming force must be deployed like the blow of a hammer—accurate, direct, and swift. It must not be used until the company is ready to put all its energy behind it. The company must also be certain that the competitive advantage it believes it has is actually available for action. On paper, the power of all a company's units may look greater than the competitor's, but can those units perform decisively together in battle?

When a company chooses the direct attack strategy, it may be necessary to completely overhaul its business in order to unleash the force. The process can feel like the turnaround of a successful company, a paradoxical situation that is uncomfortable for entrenched leaders. Only those with vision and courage should engage in this bold, and often very public, hardball strategy.

Although the force used must be massive, it is not always wise for it to be so overwhelming that you completely demolish your competitors. It may be better to keep a competitor weak and struggling than to force it into bankruptcy, from which it could emerge fit, lean, and eager for revenge. (See chapter 2.)

Exploit anomalies. Sometimes a growth opportunity lies hidden in a phenomenon that, at first glance, seems irrelevant to the business or contradictory to current practice. But anomalies—such as idiosyncratic customer preferences, unexpected employee behaviors, or odd insights from another industry—can show the way to competitive advantage, even decisive advantage.

Softball players want to ignore anomalies or try to suppress them because they don't conform to standard practice. Their senior managers usually dismiss anomalies as narrowly based or random events; running a business to meet standard operating procedures is difficult enough without having to account for every deviation that comes along.

Hardball executives, however, relish anomalies. They look for ways to exploit them, asking: What's really going on here? What can we learn from this? Is there an insight that can take our business to a whole new level?

The key to exploiting an anomaly is to expand it from a rare and isolated instance and apply it to a large volume of customers. Business processes and systems often need to be adjusted to sustain and encourage anomalous behavior and to achieve competitive advantage in cost, quality, time, and value. The reactions of competitors must be anticipated, countered, or neutralized. (See chapter 3.)

Threaten your competitor's profit sanctuaries. Profit sanctuaries are the parts of a business where a company makes the most money and steadily accumulates wealth, like a bear storing up fat for winter. In certain circumstances, the hardball player can gain competitive advantage by attacking a competitor's profit sanctuaries. This is a particularly good retaliatory strategy. If your competitor starts pushing into any of your territories, you respond by attacking his plump underbelly. He should get the message, fast.

This is also a risky strategy. It can take you deep into the caution zone, so each use must be considered on its own legal merits. Your competitor is likely to retaliate by attacking your profit sanctuaries. And he may have greater financial resources than you thought, or a "sugar daddy" waiting in the wings to save his hide. You could even face allegations of anti-competitive behavior. So, when you decide to gut the bear, it's a good idea to bring legal counsel along on the hunt. (See chapter 4.)

Take it and make it your own. Softball competitors like to think their bright ideas are sacred. Hardball players know better. They're willing to take any good idea they see (at least any one that isn't nailed down by a patent or other legal protection) and use it to create competitive advantage for themselves.

But hardball borrowing is not as easy as it may seem. It involves much more than appropriating a good idea; you have to improve on it. Harry B. Cunningham, who created Kmart in the early 1960s, admitted that Sam Walton "not only copied our concepts, he strengthened them" in his Wal-Mart stores. You also need to make the idea your own, grafting it into your organization and getting your people to buy into it. Simply replicating the details isn't enough. Just ask all the airlines that have tried and failed to copy Southwest.

You needn't restrict your borrowing to competitors. You can pick up ideas in one geographic market and transplant them in another, as Ryanair has done with Southwest's model in Europe. You can also transplant between industries, as casket maker Batesville has done. It applied the methods of the Toyota Production System to casket making and revitalized a moribund industry.

Some people might recoil when they're called a copycat. Hardball players couldn't care less. If Steve Jobs had ignored the Graphical User Interface he saw at Xerox PARC, Apple Computer would never have been born. If Kiichiro Toyoda hadn't learned just-in-time techniques from Ford, Toyota wouldn't have surpassed rival Nissan in the 1950s, much less succeeded in the United States. (See chapter 5.)

Entice your competitor into retreat. Sometimes, through a superior understanding of your business and your industry, you can take actions that confuse your competitors and entice them to behave in ways that they believe will be beneficial to them but that actually will weaken them. If you have a superb understanding of your own costs, for example, you can set prices so your competitors respond by seeking business that they think will be profitable for them, but that will, in fact, drive up their costs and depress their profits.

Enticing your competitors toward business that drives up their costs is one of the most complex and devilish strategies of hardball competition. It is a risky, bet-the-company strategy. It works best in complex businesses where costs may be misallocated. There is lots of potential for error. Your analysis of the actual versus apparent costs associated with a product, service, or customer—and the strategy that grows out of that analysis—had better be right. (See chapter 6.)

Break compromises. When a hardball player wants to achieve explosive growth, he looks for a compromise to break. A compromise is a concession that an industry forces on its customers, who often accept it because they have come to believe it is endemic—"just the way things work."

Circuit City's CarMax broke the compromise in used car retailing by offering a much bigger selection of cars of all brands and ages, simplifying the search with a computerized inventory system, and streamlining the sales process so that customers could drive away with their car in 90 minutes. CarMax has eaten the lunch of many traditional dealers and has gained the strength to beat back attacks from copycats such as Auto-Nation. (See chapter 7.)

In many cases, a company that seeks to employ one of the classic hardball strategies finds that it is not properly prepared to do so, or doesn't have all the resources it needs to get started. Sometimes the best and fastest way for a company to put itself in a position to deploy its desired hardball strategy is to acquire or merge with a company that has the needed capability or resource. Chapter 8 is a discussion of how merger and acquisition activity can be used, not as a strategy unto itself, but as a way to further a hardball strategy or strengthen a competitive advantage.

THE HARDBALL PLAYING FIELD

In these chapters, we intend to take you deep into the world of hardball competition and hardball competitors, to see who uses hardball strategies when, where, and how. Some of the stories we tell are unfolding now, others played out years ago. Several of the examples come from the automotive industry, with each story revealing a different dimension of hardball. All the stories have been selected because they are timeless, can be applied across industries (today and tomorrow), and, most of all, because they dramatically portray a classic strategy. In our telling of the stories, we hover low over the facts to give a rich sense of what it takes to play hardball.

Although the rules of hardball apply in every industry, companies are most successful with these strategies in industries where significant cost and capability advantages can be established. In capital-intensive industries—such as airlines, paper, and steel—achieving an advantage in cost or capabilities is very difficult, if not impossible. When the capital equipment is available to anyone wishing to make the investment, it is quite easy to enter the industry and become a low-cost competitor. In the airlines, for example, almost any company can buy some aircraft, hire an experienced management team, set fares low, and start flying. Such a competitor may kick up some dust for awhile, but any advantage it has will be fleeting as its competitors rush to match or beat its prices. It takes a very disciplined hardball airline competitor—such as Southwest Airlines and Ryanair—to create and sustain an advantage.

In expense-intensive industries, however, companies can invest ahead of their competitors to achieve a genuine advantage that is very difficult and expensive to replicate, if it can be replicated at all. You cannot simply buy several large stores with large parking lots and match Wal-Mart's cost and capability advantage. You cannot just purchase an auto manufacturing plant and start churning out cars as good as Toyotas. The same is true of the advantage that companies such as Victoria's Secret, Intel, and Batesville Casket Company have created for themselves. No amount of capital can buy you the advantage they have in knowledge, products, systems, locations, people, reputation, and relationships.

Companies that achieve strong competitive advantage, and especially those that go on to create decisive advantage, tend to have much longer successful runs than their competitors. There is no limit to the duration of advantage, nor is there any average lifespan we know of for advantaged companies. It is the leader that usually causes itself to lose decisive advantage, sometimes as the result of a serious mistake, but most often through complacency and failure to adapt. If a company is aggressive at renewing its competitive advantage, it may enjoy a very long run indeed, as have Wal-Mart, Microsoft, Intel, Toyota, Canon, and many others.

But, whatever industry they play in, hardball competitors cannot expect to bask in the leadership position for very long without being attacked. There are smart competitors in every business area, and it won't take them long to see your success and start trying to figure out a way to take a piece of it for themselves.

As a result, playing hardball is the toughest game in the world. Don't try to play if your management practices are sloppy. Don't expect to stay on the field long if you don't keep your edge sharp by constantly increasing your knowledge. For that, make sure you have a professional set of hardball equipment—including cost benchmarking tools, competitive tear-down skills, and a customer compromise analysis kit—to help you determine your best hardball move and develop a good sense of how your competitor might move against you. Finally, don't think you can play the game by yourself. Hardball is a team sport. You need a network of customers, suppliers, employees, and advisers whom you trust to tell you the truth.

Nor is hardball the most relaxing game you might choose to play. You want to be home by 5 P.M.? You want to clip coupons? You want to retire before China becomes a problem for your business? Nuh-uh. To play hardball, you and your organization have to go to the "heart of the matter" and stay there. You have to live by the rock face. You have to be willing to put your competitors through pain. You have to have a high energy level and the ability to sustain it. (See chapter 9.)

The world of hardball is inhabited by the brave, not the boastful. Many of the companies we describe in this book are clients of The Boston Consulting Group. Where we use their real names, we have vetted our descriptions of their stories with them. Many of the people and companies featured in the book have moved on to new places and strategies and, as a result, were not concerned about revealing information that, had it been revealed at the time, might have weakened their position. A small number of our players, however, were not yet ready to declassify their strategies for success, and so, out of respect for their desire to remain anonymous, we have disguised their identities, companies, and the industries they played in.

But all their stories are true. And all their success is here for you to use, to help you develop your own advantage, build your own virtuous cycle, and point you toward your own decisive victory.

TWO

Unleash Massive and Overwhelming Force

Although the indirect attack is the preferred hardball strategy, there are times when a company has such superior resources that it can use them to overwhelm its competitors with a direct onslaught. GM did so, in 2001, when it used its massive financial strength and low costs to offer a zero financing scheme that forced Ford and Chrysler to respond and, ultimately, did those competitors damage. In the early 1990s, Frito-Lay unleashed its extensive resources, especially its killer distribution system, to overwhelm an upstart competitor, Eagle Snacks.

Using massive and overwhelming force, however, is not as sure a bet as it may sound. The company that intends to use force must be sure it actually has the resources it thinks it has, and they must be readily accessible.

A company must also have the will to deploy its resources with sufficient commitment. It is one thing to have money in the bank, quite another to write a big check. Leaders are often reluctant to use massive force, especially when their situation is not immediately life-threatening. The urge is very strong to sit on a lead, milk a product, and stay comfortable.

The upstart competitor, bent on attack, can see when the leader or the leading player has gotten fat and sluggish. The upstart will quickly deploy its attack strategy and penetrate the leader's customer base. If the leader does not respond, the upstart pushes the attack even harder. By the time the leader notices the attack and takes it seriously, it may be too late to marshal its overwhelming resources and force the competitor into retreat. Suddenly, the upstart has the competitive advantage and the leader finds itself trying to hit hardballs with a softball bat.

GM STANDS AND FIGHTS

General Motors originally achieved decisive advantage with an indirect attack. In 1913, Ford had created competitive advantage with its production method, the assembly line, and was the leading car maker in the United States. Ford could turn out cars in higher volumes at lower cost than any competitor. Alfred P. Sloan, chairman of General Motors, decided in 1920 that the best way to challenge the leader was to offer what Ford did not: product variety. Within a decade, General Motors had pushed Ford into second place.

By the 1950s, GM dominated the economy of the United States and was the largest automotive company in the world. In 1952, Charles Wilson, chairman of General Motors, famously told a Senate committee, "for years I thought what was good for our country was good for General Motors, and vice versa." The company was highly respected, even feared.

In the 1970s, after decades of market leadership, General Motors went soft and whiny. It seemed that what had been the source of their competitive advantage—the ability to create what Alfred Sloan had called "a car for every purse and purpose"—had turned into a competitive liability. GM suffered from an overproliferation of boring, low-quality products, brand confusion, and high costs. The company's executives displayed the characteristics of the powerful but sluggish leader; they championed the status quo and quibbled about their perks. When Toyota mounted an indirect attack, they could not bring themselves to deploy the massive resources at their disposal. Down went GM's market share and the company lumbered toward bankruptcy. Experts in the car industry wrote them off.

Starting in the late 1990s, CEO Richard Smith, and then his successor CEO Rick Wagoner, worked quietly behind the scenes to change

GM. Product quality improved until it was better than Ford and Chrysler and, on some models, came close to Japanese standards. Bob Lutz, an industry veteran, was brought in to revamp GM's designs. Cadillac's bold, sharp-angled look enabled it to gain share on its traditional rival, Lincoln, and then set its sights on BMW and Mercedes.[1]

Wagoner was also able to improve GM's cash position. From 1979 to 2000, GM sold or closed thirty-five assembly, power train, and stamping plants, shifting their operations to more productive facilities. During the same period, Ford—wanting to keep peace with the labor unions and avoid a strike that might affect the all-important profit contribution from their light truck business—sold or closed only four plants. (Keeping peace is not a hardball strategy.) As a result, in 2000, for the first time in more than a decade, GM became the most productive automaker of the Big Three. Its assembly labor hours per vehicle fell below those of Ford and Chrysler and had improved at 17 percent per year. GM's cash position, superior productivity, and lower costs gave it a tremendous, readily accessible, financial resource that it could deploy whenever it chose.[2]

GM unleashed this massive force just one week after the terrorist attacks of September 11, 2001. The company announced, in an ad campaign whose theme was "Keep America Rolling," that it would offer zero percent financing on all its vehicles. Consumers took no time to realize that GM was ready to provide virtually free loans to buy their new vehicles.

Many members of the press and analyst community saw zero percent financing as a desperate move made by a floundering car company. "It's an unbearable cost for the industry, and it's unsustainable," wrote one analyst.[3] A Goldman Sachs analyst tut-tutted, "Frankly we're not that impressed because extreme and unsustainable incentives are responsible for the volume. We believe extreme price discounting is counterproductive because volume sold today at negative cash flow is volume that can't be sold tomorrow at a profit."[4]

Despite these warnings, Rick Wagoner's hardball move paid off for General Motors. Although most analysts had predicted that the auto industry would flounder in the economic aftermath of 9/11, zero percent financing caused GM's sales to rocket—they achieved 35 percent higher sales in September 2001 than in September of the year before. In fact, the entire U.S. auto industry benefited from the move and posted one of its best years ever. For the first time in more than a decade, GM gained market share.

Although the basis of GM's hardball move was the company's considerable financial resources, three other factors combined to boost that strength into a massive, overwhelming force.

First, at the time of the zero financing announcement, GM had an avalanche of new vehicles to offer. In 2000–2001, the company had launched eighteen new models, double the number of new offers from Ford and Chrysler combined. Even in a slumping market, GM's product launches took sales from Ford and Chrysler vehicles. The analysts were correct to argue that some sales would be stolen from GM's first and second quarters of 2002, but many more of them would be stolen from Ford and Chrysler.[5]

Second, GM knew its rivals were in shaky financial health and that it could sustain better than either of them the debt load resulting from zero financing. Chrysler was in the middle of its difficult merger with Daimler-Benz. Ford's profits were under extreme pressure as a result of the Firestone-Explorer rollover problem, as well as slow sales of several poor-quality vehicles. Ford's debt-to-equity ratio was almost twice that of GM's. Its cash flow available for debt service was less than GM's and the cost of incremental debt to Ford was 60 percent higher than it was to GM.

Finally, Wagoner won an emotional advantage with car buyers. Although Ford and Chrysler quickly copied the zero percent financing offer—Ford within two days and Chrysler within a week—GM had stepped out first and most aggressively. Although some saw the move as shameless exploitation of a national trauma, many gave GM credit for helping the American economy when it was at risk. This emotional benefit helped GM: Ford or Chrysler could not counter the emotions that consumers felt toward GM at that time. GM had set the agenda. (Toyota and Honda, however, did not follow it. They felt no need to join in the zero financing game in a significant way.)

Competitors claimed the move was reckless, driving the industry in the wrong direction, but GM kept it going for almost two years. Industry leaders whined all the way, begging for an end to zero percent financing and urging car makers to reduce their reliance on all sales incentives. But Rick Wagoner didn't quit and he didn't apologize. "There's been a lot of finger pointing and hand wringing," he said. "We're going to keep playing the game. The strategy is working for us." It is better, he said, than, "wishing and whining ourselves into a recession."[6] Not only did the strategy work for GM, it seriously weakened its competitors. Ford, largely because it had to match GM's zero percent financing for so long, saw its S&P bond rating drop to near-junk status. This is particularly ominous since Ford is a major issuer of corporate bonds.

GM still has a great distance to go to match Toyota's strength in the car business, but keeping Ford and Chrysler on the ropes certainly helps.

FRITO-LAY USES MASSIVE DISTRIBUTION FORCE TO OVERWHELM A SNEAK ATTACK

Salty snacks—such as potato chips, corn chips, tortilla chips, and pretzels—might seem like a softball business, but the supermarket can be a very tough place to play. Although Frito-Lay is currently a cash machine for its parent, PepsiCo, with 60 percent share of the salty snack category and greater than 50 percent gross margins, it came perilously close to losing its leadership in the 1990s when Eagle Snacks swooped in with an indirect attack.[7]

Frito-Lay had long held a decisive advantage in "salties," as industry insiders call salty snacks, which stemmed from the superior route economics of its store door delivery system (SDD)—the process of getting fresh products from the factory to the store and merchandising them there. It is an onerous logistical challenge to deliver fresh (and fragile) product, in fairly small numbers of units, directly to the doors of a very large number of retail outlets, rather than make a smaller number of large shipments to the loading docks of wholesalers or big retailers' warehouses. The company has been perfecting the system since 1961, when the leading corn chip brand (Fritos) and the leading potato chip brand (Lays) were merged to create Frito-Lay. Early on, it learned to invest its dollars where the customer shops.

The key drivers of cost in the store door delivery system are the drop size (size of the shipment), route density (how many retail outlets on a distribution route), system efficiency (speed of loading and unloading, order fulfillment, amount of breakage), speed of turns in the retail store, and the cost of the route rep. Frito-Lay chose to pay its reps better than its competitors, so that cost was higher than average. But the company created a significant advantage on the other costs, which amounted to as much as 15 cents on every $1 bag of salty snacks.

This advantage in route economics triggered a virtuous cycle for Frito-Lay. It had more profits than its competitors, giving it more money to invest in product quality and consumer advertising, while still dropping a good deal of profit to the bottom line. These investments helped Frito-Lay sell more chips, which further improved its route economics, generating more profits to fund more advertising, and so on. Frito-Lay's competitors were at a disadvantage, which put them into a negative cycle. They sold fewer chips. Their route economics got worse. They had less money to spend on product and advertising. It seemed impossible to catch Frito-Lay.

By the late 1980s, Frito-Lay had more than ten thousand reps servicing more than 325,000 supermarkets, mass merchants, convenience stores, and vending machines. The reps stocked the retailers' stores and got their products the most favorable placement in the aisle and on the shelf. They "popped" the bags so that the Frito-Lay products looked more appealing than competitors' bags. The formula worked exceptionally well. Some grocery outlets in the southwestern United States sold so much Frito-Lay product that the company could afford to dedicate a full-time sales rep to each store to ensure the shelves were always properly stocked and merchandised.

Over the years, Frito-Lay parlayed its advantage into decisive advantage, earning high profits and high market share.

Frito-Lay's competitors, frustrated at their inability to break Frito-Lay's virtuous cycle, turned to softball tactics. They tipped off legislators about an industry practice known as "slotting fees"—money paid by a manufacturer to a retailer to place a new product on the shelf. (In fact, the trade promotion money that manufacturers provide to large supermarket chains accounts for more than 100 percent of the chains' total profits.) The Justice Department launched an investigation, but found that no laws had been broken.

This softball tactic only succeeded in proving that Frito-Lay, although playing hardball, was abiding by the rules.

THE SLIDE TO SOFTBALL

Over the years, Frito-Lay added several more hit brands, including Ruffles and Doritos, to their line, but eventually the company's growth slowed. Looking for a new source of sales and profit they decided to expand into a different type of product: cookies and crackers.

Unfortunately, Frito-Lay's finely tuned store door delivery system, which was so efficient in the handling of fresh and fragile product, was not suited to cookies and crackers. They are a hardier breed of snack, less susceptible to breakage and more capable of withstanding time on the pallet at the warehouse. Frito-Lay's store door delivery system, which was designed for quick delivery of small shipments to multiple locations, was too expensive for the distribution of cookies and crackers.

Frito-Lay struggled to gain momentum with cookies and crackers. The route reps were frustrated because cookies and crackers took up valuable space in their trucks, but did not turn on the shelves as fast as salties, and were thus less profitable. Plus, the new lines meant more work for the reps; they had to manage three times more shelf space than they had before, although the new products added less than 20 percent in sales volume. Sales, general, and administration costs went up. To cover losses made on the cookie and cracker lines, management dramatically raised prices on salty snacks and launched several new products that turned out to be duds. Remember O'Gradys Au Gratin flavored thick-ridged potato chips? Probably not.

But, like the 1980s managers at GM, Frito-Lay executives were in denial. The company moved into a lavish new headquarters building in Dallas, complete with executive dining rooms, a health club, and a man-made lake. It might as well have had a softball field, too.

Enter Anheuser-Busch (A-B). With its powerhouse beer brands—Budweiser, Michelob, and Busch—A-B was every bit as strong in the U.S. beer market as Frito-Lay was in the salty snack market. Their market share was nearly 40 percent; they had presence in the vast majority of stores, restaurants, and bars that offered their product categories; their distributors were powerful and profitable.

A-B had a small salty snack business, primarily in honey-roasted peanuts. With Frito-Lay distracted by cookies and stumbling in salty snacks, A-B saw an opening to make a foray into a big, high-margin business that had only one truly national player. A-B had a strong beer distribution system they thought they could use against Frito-Lay. Their route density in supermarkets was as good as Frito-Lay's and it was nearly as good for small retailers. Besides, salty snacks and beer is a great product and consumer fit.

Anheuser-Busch launched Eagle brand in 1982 and the brand had nationwide exposure by 1989, offering potato chips, corn chips, and pretzels along with their honey-roasted peanuts.

Eagle pursued a brilliant indirect strategy. With the help of many ex-Frito-Lay sales and marketing executives hired expressly to take the fight to Frito-Lay, it decided not to attack Frito-Lay at the center of its business: supermarkets. Instead, Eagle made raids at the outposts. It placed Eagle snacks with the airlines to generate trials. (Seasoned fliers will remember those little bags of Eagle honey-roasted peanuts.) They sold into bars and taverns, where the natural product fit gave them instant acceptance. These early trials established Eagle as a high-quality brand. Then Eagle took aim at smaller supermarkets and grocery outlets where Frito-Lay had less clout than with the big accounts. And Eagle began to advertise. Unlike Frito-Lay, which has a unique brand name for each of its products, Eagle leveraged its one brand name across its entire line. It could promote all its products with one brand campaign, saving millions on advertising.

Eagle's attack exposed another Frito-Lay weakness: the quality of its potato chips. Potato chips were much less profitable for Frito-Lay than Doritos and Fritos, its corn products. With its profits lagging from the misadventure into cookies and crackers, Frito-Lay had been reluctant to invest in improving the quality of its potato chips. Now, in blind taste tests, consumers said that Eagle brand potato chips tasted better than Lays. Even more distressing, Lays potato chips scored even lower in taste tests when the brand names were revealed. That meant that consumers not only had problems with the taste of the product, they also had negative feelings about the brand. Lays began to lose market share.

At Frito-Lay headquarters in Plano, Texas, a discussion began about whether it would be more financially painful to lose share in potato chips or to invest in improving their quality. As Eagle steadily picked up share, the discussions escalated into arguments. Eagle was not only succeeding in the marketplace, it was creating confusion inside the enemy's camp.

Eagle knew what it was doing. The company, in a "take it and make it your own" move, had hired many former Frito-Lay employees to staff its product development operations, run its manufacturing plants, and manage its marketing activities. These Eagle managers knew Frito-Lay's processes as well as, if not better than Frito-Lay's own staffers. In fact, the Eagle managers had more combined years of experience working for Frito-Lay than did the Frito-Lay management team, which enabled Eagle to respond to Frito-Lay's moves faster and more effectively than they might have otherwise. For example, if Frito-Lay introduced a new potato product, Eagle could copy it and have it in stores four weeks later, a remarkably quick response.

By 1991, Eagle had grabbed 6 percent share in the salty snack market. Anheuser-Busch declared it was committed to the business for the long haul and set ambitious growth objectives for their exciting new brand.

Then Eagle made a bold, but ultimately fatal, move. It decided to make a direct attack on Frito-Lay. It chose to launch a tortilla product to compete with Doritos. Doritos was, and still is, Frito-Lay's largest brand. It is PepsiCo's most profitable brand globally and the corporation's single most valuable asset.

But Doritos was just too tempting a target for Eagle. From their own experience within Frito-Lay, Eagle's management knew how profitable Doritos was for their rival. The Eagle managers analyzed how much money their company would make, market by market, if they could capture a share in tortilla chips similar to the share they had grabbed in potato chips, and it was a lot. Most important, the management team realized that Doritos was Frito-Lay's profit sanctuary and that Frito-Lay could, at any moment, choose to use its enormous profits from tortilla chips to crush Eagle's potato chip attack. As long as Frito-Lay was as strong as it was, Eagle would be vulnerable.

If Eagle had continued to play at the edges of Frito-Lay's financial heartland, it might have gradually built its position and become very hard to dislodge. Frito-Lay might even have decided that it made more sense to cede share in potato chips than to improve quality and allowed A-B to achieve competitive advantage there. Instead, the direct attack on Doritos awoke the giant.

FRITO-LAY RENEWS ITS COMPETITIVE ADVANTAGE

PepsiCo brought in its best talent to respond to the Doritos threat. In January 1991, Roger Enrico took over as CEO of Frito-Lay. He had won fame in the Pepsi-versus-Coke Cola Wars, during which he had convinced the world that Pepsi tasted better. As a result, Pepsi became the leading soft drink in U.S. supermarkets. Enrico knew how to play hardball and he understood the playing field.

Enrico worried that if Eagle were allowed to gain 10 percent market share in salty snacks, the upstart competitor would start to benefit from the virtuous loop that Frito-Lay had enjoyed for so long. Enrico could not allow A-B to establish such a position. But how to return Frito-Lay to hardball? Where to start?

Despite Eagle's success, Frito-Lay had been so successful for so long that it had largely been able to gloss over the signs of damage and ignore the growing threat. Apart from the potato chip debates, it had been easy to dismiss the danger. Yet Enrico knew that decisive advantage can be as fragile as a potato chip. Frito-Lay had taken one misstep into the cookie aisle. Another might lead to disaster. Enrico's job was to make the company truly believe it was in danger and get it to respond. He faced one of the most difficult of corporate challenges: turning around a successful company.

Enrico began by carefully studying his new company, and concluded that Frito-Lay was fundamentally a very fine organization. "We had terrific people," he said. "We were functionally excellent. People were motivated." The problem was that "everybody was doing a superb job on stuff that didn't mean anything."

Even so, it was very difficult to convince his team, and even his board of directors, that Eagle represented a serious threat. "One of the directors said to me, 'Why create this battle mentality against Eagle, when they only have a 6 percent share?' I said to him, 'Market share only moves in two directions. Up or down. Ours is going down.'" Enrico talked about the 1950s, when Coke had seven times the market share of Pepsi. "Don't you think that if Coke could relive the 1950s, they'd do things differently?" he asked.

Some of the management complacency came from Frito-Lay's past success at beating back any rival that dared set foot on its salty turf.

Frito-Lay had vanquished insurgent products from other giants, including General Mills, Procter & Gamble, and General Foods. "But Anheuser-Busch was different," said Enrico. "They knew how to work the supermarket aisles. They knew quality and manufacturing. They were great marketers. And they had cash flow to burn."

These past successes had created a number of beliefs within the Frito-Lay organization. "We thought that our quality was the best. It wasn't," said Enrico. "We thought that nobody could beat us at distribution. But I knew they could." Enrico couldn't get his people to understand that the loss of eight share points was significant. "I'd be at a meeting in the plant and everybody would look at me like I was from Mars," said Enrico. "Finally, the head of manufacturing told me that the organization only responded to things that 'make the building shake.' If they missed the monthly profit target, that made the building shake. But loss of market share didn't cause a murmur."

So Enrico realized he had to make the danger sound real and imminent. In a major speech, Enrico told his people that the organization was caught in the "tyranny of incrementalism." To beat back the Eagle challenge and regain Frito-Lay's edge in quality, it would be necessary to make "big changes on big things." Making small changes on big things is dangerous. You feel like you're making progress when you aren't. Small changes on small things are just a waste of time.

Enrico defined four big things that needed big changes. He urged his people to:

- Make quality a reality.
- Take back the streets.
- Find a better way.
- Win together.

Enrico focused first on the customer experience—"making quality a reality." But it was not easy to change an organization that thought it was producing good quality potato chips. On a visit to a manufacturing facility, he asked one of the operators of a potato fryer, "What makes a good potato chip?" She replied, "I do." Enrico realized that there were no clear or consistent criteria for defining a good chip. Plus, the quality systems at the plants were all reporting that quality was fine. "The quality reports all said that everything was 99.9 percent perfect," said Enrico.

The problem was, however, that the systems were averaging the results for six different characteristics. One could be substantially off and it would not significantly affect the report.

Enrico and his team created a "gold standard" potato chip—product that exhibited the optimal qualities of the finest potato chip. Each month they would send a bag of the gold standard chips to the manufacturing facilities. When the gold standard chips arrived, the plant managers and line workers would get together at the end of a shift and look at them, analyze them, and compare them to the product that was currently coming off the line. They would also study the chips of their competitors.

They also created a consumer panel for each plant, composed of outsiders who would come in to the plant and rate the Frito-Lay chips in comparison to the competition. "The plant people hated this," said Enrico. "They hated being compared and coming out worse than the competitors." It didn't take long for the plant people to get a jump on the process. They would go out and buy competitive product to analyze it themselves, before the consumer panel convened, and adjust their process to make Lays better than the best brand available. Pretty soon, the Lays manufacturing facilities were deeply involved with quality, with regular taste tests and a "wall of quality" that displayed their results and achievements.

Enrico and his team kept a close eye on the quality efforts. Once a week, products made by all of Frito-Lay's facilities—Fritos, Lays, Doritos, Cheetos—were delivered to Enrico's office. Enrico and his team would taste and evaluate each sample. They became expert at evaluating the qualitative elements of the product. Is the curl right? Are the chips standard length? Is the color golden brown? Is the taste just right? "I developed a pretty good palate for salties," Enrico said.

Often, they found problems. Some batches of Fritos corn chips, for example, had an undesirable "mouth feel"—no delightful snap or salty zing. He discovered that some plants, to save money, were skimping on ingredients. The corn chip recipe called for oil content to be 18 to 20 percent of total product weight, but some plants were reducing oil content to reduce costs. This did indeed reduce cost, but it also reduced the taste appeal. When Enrico discovered a product that he considered inferior, he called the plant manager directly to express his dissatisfaction.

The gold standards, quality efforts, and personal attention improved quality, but not enough for Enrico. Frito-Lay planned to make a major relaunch of Lays potato chips, featuring new advertising that would premiere during the Super Bowl in January. Winter is not the best time for making potato chips, because it is not potato season, and the quality of the raw materials entering the plants is not as high as it is in the summer. But Enrico chose to relaunch in the winter for that very reason— to dramatize the difference between the taste of a gold standard Lays potato chip and the taste of a competitive chip in its winter doldrums. As the relaunch approached, product quality was still not good enough and Enrico asked for a higher standard from his manufacturing people. They adjusted their automated quality monitoring systems so that more product was rejected, but it was still letting bad product through. "You guys don't understand," Enrico told his manufacturing managers. He got them to tune the system so it would reject everything but gold standard product. They did, and it resulted in the rejection of some $30 million of product. There were lots of cattle that winter that ate more than their fill of Lays potato chips.

"I knew this would drive the plant guys crazy," said Enrico. The manufacturing managers hated to reject product and couldn't tolerate inefficiencies in their plants. So they worked out a new potato purchasing system. Instead of buying from wholesalers, they contracted directly with potato farmers and made the farmers responsible for quality.

Even while Enrico insisted that there should be no skimping on the cost of product quality, he looked for ways to cut administrative costs. In 1991, he restructured the organization, with the intention of removing $100 million in costs. He needed flexibility on pricing and had to stop relying on inflated margins from salty snacks to cover the organization's bloated costs. He cut 25 percent of Frito-Lay's managerial and administrative jobs. A risky move, many said. Cut too much, too close to the bone, and the organization's ability to innovate would be stripped away for at least five years. Don't cut enough and its ability to compete will still be compromised, because of the high cost structure. Others criticized the move, saying that Enrico was cutting costs just so he could make his profit target for the year. "But we spent the whole $100 million on improving the business. The first year, we didn't hit our profit target. But we did grow the top line."

Enrico also worked on the second big change, taking back the streets. He refocused the organization on its main competitive advantage: its massive force in salty snack distribution. He killed the large packages of cookies and crackers, retaining only the single-serve items. He reduced by 30 percent the number of stock keeping units (SKUs) in the entire Frito-Lay product line. This dramatically changed the life of the route reps and returned them to the ways that had built their success. Ten thousand route reps were freed to put all their energy into salty snack distribution. Once again, they could fill the trucks with fast-moving items only. They had fewer stales to pick up. They could allocate more space to the fastest-moving items, reducing out-of-stocks.

Enrico also was successful in the third big thing—finding a better way, especially in functional practices. As a marketing professional, he was eager to redirect the company's marketing energy to salty snacks. He found that Frito-Lay had established seven regional marketing operations so that brand marketing people could provide better promotional and merchandising support to the major retailers, such as Safeway grocery stores. But, over time, these regional marketing units had also been allocated funds for consumer marketing, including advertising, as a way to grow sales in their regions for individual products and brands. This was an activity that Enrico realized was a small move on a big thing. "Marketing in the field is a joke," he said. "The field can't get to the deep consumer insights." As a result, the local campaigns never had enough force or impact to break through the national advertising clutter. Such spending became known throughout the company as "bunny marketing." (Anything with "bunny" as its descriptor can be considered a small move.) In one fell swoop, Enrico abolished all bunny marketing. He decided that the consumer should be the exclusive focus of headquarters. Regional marketing operations would return to their original role of giving the retailer whatever support they could. "We put the field in charge of the profit plan and headquarters in charge of the balance sheet."

Enrico also found a big cost drain, time sink, and barrier to innovation in Frito's product management process. Whenever a change or innovation was proposed—in packaging, flavor, or pricing, for example—the brand team had to go through an elaborate process known as 2227. (This was the number of the internal form that had to be used to gain approval.) The nature of the change and the rationale for it had to be described, and then there were twelve signature lines, one each for twelve functional managers. Without twelve signatures on the form, the change was dead. The process had been created to ensure that all functions were informed about changes coming to market, but it had become a bureaucracy unto itself, best suited to saying no. The 2227 process had been in place for more than a decade; there were full-time employees whose sole responsibility it was to manage it.

Enrico blew up the whole thing. In its place, he established a new product management process. The brand team worked together to create a marketing calendar for the quarter, including all promotions, specials, and packaging and product changes or introductions. The functions then had to collaborate with the store door delivery system to execute flawlessly.

TAKING AIM AT ANHEUSER-BUSCH

Enrico's internal moves amounted to a major overhaul of the company, which was necessary to ensure that Frito-Lay's resources were in fighting trim and available to be deployed. "We had a much bigger 'capability share' than we did market share," he said. "We must have had 90 percent of the R&D talent in the industry. 80 percent of the marketing talent. But we only had 40 percent share of the market. We were seriously under leveraging our capabilities. We were optimizing everything, but leveraging nothing."

But now, with distractions removed, salty snack product quality up, costs under control, and processes fine-tuned, Enrico could unleash the massive and overwhelming force of the Frito-Lay product development and marketing capabilities, and especially the power of its distribution system, ten thousand route reps strong.

To support the attack, Enrico had two hardball tricks up his sleeve. First, he cut prices. This caught competitors by surprise. During the previous decade, Frito-Lay had led industry prices up, first to match or outpace inflation, and then to cover the costs of failed or poor-performing new products. Frito-Lay's competitors had grown accustomed to the price umbrella and felt comfortable in its shelter. Even if their cost structure was much higher than Frito-Lay's, they could still undercut the leader's price and make a profit.

Enrico snapped the umbrella shut. Many competitors got wet. Regional players such as Granny Goose, Cains, and Borden shut their doors within three years. As a result, Frito regained market share. This was a hardball move, played near the caution zone without actually entering it. It was aggressive pricing, but not predatory pricing. The price cuts were made across all products to all retailers in all regions, rather than aimed at specific competitors in specific situations.

Enrico also had a special surprise for Eagle. According to Steve Englander, then Eagle's head of marketing, "Frito-Lay could never figure out the chink in the Eagle armor. When they figured it out, it did not take long for Frito to make Eagle go away."[8]

Enrico knew that it would not make sense to attack Eagle on product quality, because Frito might lose. Nor could Frito-Lay necessarily beat Eagle with advertising, because the Eagle brand was now well-established and well-respected. Enrico concluded that he would combine two hardball strategies—unleash Frito's massive force to devastate Eagle's primary profit sanctuary, the supermarket business. Without that profit sanctuary, Eagle's business would be untenable, because they could not survive by supplying airlines and bars. Thanks to the internal overhaul, Enrico's route reps effectively had 30 percent more time to spend on selling and distributing salty snacks—the equivalent of adding nine hundred new people. Frito-Lay struck hard to take back the street from Eagle.

Enrico tapped into his people's will to win. He had doormats made that featured the Eagle Snacks eagle logo overlaid with the "not" symbol (the circle sliced through with a diagonal slash). At the annual Frito-Lay conference, the mats were placed at the entrance to every room so people could tromp on the Eagle. People throughout the organization created their own versions of the "stressed Eagle." Like fighter jet pilots, machine operators would stick them on the side of their machines as they worked to create product that would beat Eagle in the monthly taste tests. The route drivers displayed the stressed Eagle on the doors of their trucks, as they went about the business of stocking stores and shocking Eagle.

Enrico also played a bit of corporate hardball with Anheuser-Busch. At the time, PepsiCo manufactured and supplied beverage cans to its rival. And Pizza Hut, a PepsiCo company, served Budweiser beer in their outlets. Enrico put pressure on Pepsi's chairman, Wayne Calloway, to sever these relationships with Anheuser-Busch.

Although Roger Enrico left Frito-Lay in 1993 to become vice-chairman of PepsiCo, his successor, Steve Reinemund, pursued the massive force strategy with just as much determination and even higher goals. As Reinemund was preparing to take the helm at Frito-Lay he spent two months in the field visiting customers, the sales force, and manufacturing and distribution sites, and talking with consumers. Reinemund came away convinced that Enrico had put together a brilliant strategy, but that even more could be done with it. "I had been happy with 7–8 percent sales growth," said Enrico. "Steve said he thought he could deliver double digit growth." Enrico doubted it was possible, but Reinemund made good on his promise. It was bad news for Eagle.

In the end, Eagle was unable to withstand Frito-Lay's overwhelming force that was composed of improved quality product, lower prices, and the bulked-up distribution organization, and further strengthened by the pressure put on Eagle by PepsiCo through Eagle's parent, Anheuser-Busch. By 1996, Frito-Lay had gained back four share points, stopping Eagle Brands in its tracks. After Anheuser-Busch closed the doors on Eagle, Frito-Lay purchased four of its factories.

The Frito-Lay story is one of an impressive, decisive, and classic use of massive force.

WHEN USING FORCE, USE CAUTION

The use of force can sometimes backfire. It can be a dangerous strategy, for example, if the company deploying it does not have a cost advantage over its competitors, and does not have at least product parity and, preferably, product advantage, as well. Without those advantages, competitors can blunt the forceful attack with attractive, new customer offers, better products, or price cuts.

The use of force can also go too far, creating undesirable consequences for the attacker. If the force is so overwhelming that the competitor ends up as roadkill, it may be able to take cover in bankruptcy protection. Then it will have the time and ability to renegotiate contracts on favorable terms and shed unproductive assets. It may emerge from bankruptcy fitter and leaner than ever, ready to fight back or make its own indirect attack. It's often best to use just enough force to weaken a competitor, but not obliterate it.

Finally, the market leader that deploys massive strength is a natural target for competitive protest, bad press, and legal investigation. Overwhelming force is an appropriate strategy only for the company that is willing to take the time to gather good market intelligence and make a plan that avoids any taint of the abuse of market power. If you are charged with wrongdoing, even if you are eventually found innocent, defending against a legal action is its own form of distraction, can eat up resources, and can have a negative impact on a brand's reputation. Don't let that happen.

But, for the company that has powerful resources, is capable of tuning them into fighting trim, has the will to deploy them, and the self-restraint to avoid bully behavior, the use of massive and overwhelming force is certainly one of the most effective hardball strategies and probably the most exciting to watch and participate in.

"It was a lot of fun," said Roger Enrico. "It was absolutely the finest moment of my career."

THREE

Exploit Anomalies

Sometimes a growth opportunity lies hidden in something—such as an idiosyncratic customer preference or a seemingly aberrant employee behavior—that, at first glance, seems to have no relevance to strategy, the business, or growth. Hardball players know that such anomalies can contain the seeds of a new business idea, and they look for ways to exploit them.

An anomaly is an irregularity, a departure from the norm. A good example of a business anomaly is the one identified by a guy named Joe Girard. According to the *Guinness World Records,* Girard is the world's greatest automobile salesman, as measured by volume. Harry Beckwith calls him "the Michelangelo and Tiger Woods of sales."[1] In Girard's book *How to $ell Anything to Anybody* he describes what he calls the "Rule of 250," which states that everybody in the world knows at least 250 people with whom they have some degree of influence. The Rule of 250 is the basis for Joe's approach to selling. His method is to identify people—such as a union boss, a community leader, or a well-known businessperson—who have particularly strong influence with their 250 friends and acquaintances and do everything it takes to turn those people into satisfied customers. They will do much of Joe's work of selling for him.[2]

Joe derived his Rule of 250 from an anomaly he encountered while attending a funeral in Detroit. At the funeral home, each mourner received a prayer card. Unlike every other funeral Joe had ever attended, the cards had been printed with a photograph of the deceased. As a salesman, Joe could not help wondering about the economics of these cards. They would certainly cost more to produce than a card without a photograph and, obviously, they could not be reused. Joe wondered how the funeral director decided how many cards to print—to avoid printing too few, which would be awkward, or printing too many, which would waste money. After the funeral, Joe approached the director and asked him how he determined the print quantity. The director told Joe that he had observed, in his many years of running funerals for all kinds of people, that about 250 people signed the register every time.

The anomaly of the prayer cards impressed Joe, and he concluded that if 250 people come to a person's funeral he must have had some degree of influence over them in life—perhaps enough to suggest what type of car to buy or whom to buy it from. After that funeral, Joe began to think of each prospect, not as a just as a customer, but as a window onto an additional 250 prospects. It is this attitude, he says, that has made him the world's most prolific car salesman.

Such can be the power of an anomaly found and exploited.

Most anomalies go unnoticed, however, or are ignored. Organizations try to contain or suppress them, precisely because they are departures from the norm and to embrace them might disrupt standard operating procedures. When senior managers learn of anomalies, they generally dismiss them as narrowly based, or random, one-time events. Running a business is difficult enough without having to consider and account for every seemingly random deviation encountered.

That's too bad. Anomalies can sometimes reveal what your customers really want from you. They can also provide a glimpse of what your organization is capable of achieving. Paying attention to anomalies may point you to major opportunities to grow your business by doing on a broad scale what you are already doing in some aberrant nook or cranny.

Exploiting an anomaly can be difficult—taking a limited phenomenon to a much larger scale may require that business processes and systems be adjusted in order to sustain and encourage the new behavior and to achieve competitive advantage in cost, quality, time, and value.

But, hardball executives do not ignore or dismiss anomalies. They dig into them and look for ways to exploit them, asking: What's really going on? How can we learn from this? Is there an insight buried here that can move the business to a whole new level?

WAUSAU PAPERS SEEKS TO GROW ITS SPECIALTY PAPER BUSINESS

Wausau Papers was a sleepy player in the paper industry. The company had been founded in 1899 and operated a manufacturing facility on the Wisconsin River, in the town of Brokaw in northern Wisconsin. In 1977, Richard Radt (pronounced "rod") was named president of Wausau Papers and charged by the board of directors with bringing Wausau up-to-date. It was obvious to Radt, who had been head of the paper division of Philip Morris, that the main problem at Wausau was inertia. "We were standing before an ever-moving avalanche which seemed poised to engulf us," he said. "Change was in order. And change we did."[3]

Radt began by reenergizing the core unit of the company, the Brokaw division, which made printing and writing papers. Brokaw sold its products to large paper merchants throughout the Midwest. The merchants, in turn, supplied printers and paper retailers. Through a combination of cost-cutting, quality and process improvement, and some capital investment, Radt quickly transformed Brokaw into the leading profit center for Wausau.

Radt, who was a man of action and great energy (he had been a Korean War fighter pilot and liked racing cars), next sought to grow the Brokaw division. The Brokaw plant, built in 1899, had been updated through the years, but was relatively small in comparison to its big papermaking competitors, and its machinery and processes could not match their volume and speed. However, Brokaw had a reputation for making high-quality papers and had the capability for producing them in a wide range of colors. Although there was a strong, steady demand for Brokaw's quality, colored papers, the bigger merchants preferred to deal with the bread-and-butter of the paper business—white paper, and a small number of standard colors, in reams of a few standard sizes. As a result, Brokaw generally created an exclusive relationship with just one big merchant that agreed to handle its products in that market. It would also sell through several smaller merchants.

As they were considering ways to create growth, Radt and his advisors noticed an anomaly. In Chicago, Brokaw had a much higher share than in any other market. Although Radt's management team knew about the anomaly, they had never investigated it. The vice-president of sales believed that the higher share was the result of a special particularly strong relationship between the Brokaw salesman in Chicago and the local merchants.

That was not, in fact, the case. There were two main differences in the way Brokaw did business in Chicago. First, it had relationships with most of the major paper merchants, rather than an exclusive arrangement with just one, as was its practice in other markets. Second, it delivered its products to merchants much faster than anywhere else—often the day after the order had been received. Radt wondered if this anomaly could be exploited in other markets to increase share. If so, what level of service would Brokaw need to provide? What systems and processes would need to be changed? How would the change affect costs and pricing? What might the competition do in response?

The first task was to find out what was really going on. How was it that Brokaw could deal with so many big merchants in Chicago? And how was it that it could make next-day deliveries there? The answer to the first question was that it was a fluke of history; that's just how things, over time, had developed there. But if it was possible in Chicago, why wouldn't it be possible elsewhere? The answer to the second question was that Chicago was only one hundred miles from the Brokaw plant and, what's more, almost every delivery route to the Midwestern cities served by Brokaw ran through the city. Brokaw trucks were driving through Chicago every day on the way to Kansas City or St. Louis or Minneapolis. As a result, Chicago merchants had learned that, if they placed an order with Brokaw, there was a good chance that it would get on a truck leaving the plant the next day. And the Brokaw logistics people became accustomed to throwing a Chicago order on a truck bound for Cleveland. Because the merchants knew they could get supply from Brokaw quickly, they were able to keep smaller inventories, which gave them more space to keep a much wider range of papers in inventory. This enabled them to turn their inventory more quickly and to provide a better selection and faster service to their customers. Brokaw had a bigger share in Chicago because they were helping the merchants reduce their costs and increase volume.

Once they understood the cause of the anomaly, Radt and some members of his team became convinced that they could dramatically improve Brokaw's performance if they could replicate the Chicago model in other markets. But it wouldn't be easy. There were many questions in need of answers. To find them, they would have to push themselves and their colleagues well outside their comfort zone.

They began by surveying some of Brokaw's customers beyond the Chicago area to determine the levels of service they were getting. Radt was surprised and pleased at what they found. The merchants were getting poor service from all their suppliers. Typically, the merchant had to wait one to two weeks for a delivery of a standard product, such as white printing paper. The order fulfillment rate was also mediocre; on average, 20 percent of the ordered items were missing or on back order. Not only did this hurt the merchant through lost sales, it added to his administrative cost and hassle. He had to keep track of what had been delivered and what was missing, follow up with the supplier, notify customers of the status of their orders, and make sure his accounting was accurate regarding what had been paid for and what had not.

The merchants had even more problems and complexities when it came to service on specialty products. The end customers, usually printers, liked the specialty papers because they came in such a broad range of colors and finishes. Even though the merchants disliked stocking the specialty papers, they liked specialty orders because they earned higher margins. But for the big manufacturers, Brokaw's competitors, each specialty run required a changeover, adding both cost and complexity to their process. As a result, the manufacturer usually required a minimum quantity on a specialty order, often a full truckload (forty thousand pounds of paper), and delivery took four to six weeks.

These conditions on specialty orders put the merchant in a tough position. If the customer wanted to order a small quantity of a specialty item, the merchant might be forced to take the manufacturer's minimum quantity (the truckload) and inventory the excess. But the inventory turns for specialty products were only four or five per year, compared with ten to twelve turns for standard product inventories. Plus, specialty products took up valuable storage space. So, although merchants earned a higher margin on the specialty order itself, they had come to believe that the higher margins did not add much, if anything, to their bottom line.

So Radt came to see that the small size and specialty focus of the Brokaw plant could be a competitive advantage, rather than a limitation, against the bigger manufacturers. The Brokaw plant, although outmatched by competitors when it came to big runs of standard papers, was far more suited to short, specialty runs. It was prohibitively expensive, if not out of the question, for competitors to change over their mammoth, high-speed, high-capacity machines for many kinds of small-quantity special orders. Radt began to see that a combination of fast service and specialty orders might give them an advantage the competition couldn't and wouldn't attack.

Radt decided to test the new model by running a pilot in Minneapolis. Brokaw would build up inventory of its papers and hold the inventory at the plant. It would offer next-day delivery on products already in stock. If an order came in by 4 P.M., it would arrive at the merchant's loading dock by 8 A.M. the next morning. "We told everybody that," said one of Radt's team members. "We told everybody in town."

Brokaw would also go for a dramatic improvement in order fulfillment. It set a target that every order would be 96 percent complete or better. For products not in stock, Brokaw would cut the average delivery to two weeks, down from the usual four to six weeks. Plus, they would not require the merchant to take an entire truckload.

Then Radt's team looked at pricing. They decided to offer their specialty products at the same price as their competitors, which was at about a 35 percent premium to the standard products. But they also chose to raise the price of their standard products by an average of 10 percent. By doing so, Brokaw hoped to discourage merchants from purchasing large quantities of standard products from them, simply because they wanted to devote most of their capacity to the specialty papers. They figured that this would give more of the standard business to their competitors and discourage them from competing on specialty orders. Everybody would be happy.

Finally, Radt realized that Brokaw could not afford to offer one-day turnaround and daily delivery in a market if it delivered to one merchant only. The shipping costs would be prohibitive. Therefore, it would have to end the exclusive relationships it had with big merchants in each market and sell to anyone who wanted to buy.

PREPARING TO EXECUTE THE STRATEGY

Before starting the Minneapolis pilot, Brokaw needed to make some improvements to its value delivery system, starting with production. Although the plant was already producing high-quality product quite efficiently, Radt wanted his company to get even better at rapid change-overs, color matching, paper cutting and packaging, and reducing waste. To do so, Brokaw installed additional computerized process-control systems and added new finishing lines. It became one of the smallest paper plants in the country to have so much sophisticated process-control capability.

These process improvements, which required only a small capital investment, dramatically changed the capability of the Brokaw plant. It now could offer 235 product variations to its customers. Many of them could be delivered the next day. The rest could be guaranteed to arrive within two weeks. No competitor offered more than fifty-five variations. Most promised delivery in four weeks.

Even this new production capability would not be enough to ensure fast delivery, however; quick order turnaround required quick order processing, which proved to be another Brokaw bottleneck. The company used a manual order entry procedure that was complex, time-consuming, and prone to error. If it was to keep its next-day delivery promise, orders had to be processed in minutes, not hours or days. So, Brokaw first streamlined the order-management process and then computerized it. (This is the proper order of action. Many companies computerize a faulty process and then, when the automated version fails to have a positive impact, they streamline it.)

Brokaw's logistics also needed attention. Although the logistics function appeared to be in good shape, with its fleet of late-model trucks and full-time drivers, some aspects did not lend themselves to the one-day delivery policy. Standard practice for Brokaw was to dispatch a truck only when it was full of product, and it could take days to gather enough orders to do so. Sometimes the shipping department had to deal with the opposite problem; a distributor would place such a big order that Brokaw ran out of truck capacity and had to send a partial order or make two runs. In addition, when a truck had to travel more than four hundred miles, the driver was required by law to make an eight-hour rest stop.

In order to keep the next-day delivery promise, Brokaw would have to place more importance on the customer order than on full trucks. So, starting with the Minneapolis trial, it abandoned the "no truck leaves half-full" motto. It allowed trucks to be scheduled as needed. It empowered the shipping department to lease trucks when needed to handle very large orders. For long hauls, it assigned two drivers to one truck so it could make next-day deliveries to distributors beyond the four-hundred-mile limit. For smaller orders, if no truck was available, the shipping department was authorized to use an overnight delivery service, such as FedEx or UPS, if the customer would not wait an extra day.

It is one thing, of course, to put new processes in place and quite another to get people to use them at all, let alone with efficiency and conviction. Radt faced a difficult challenge in changing the mind-set of the people in his organization.

The director of logistics, for example, could not bring himself to release a truck if it wasn't full or close to it. He had spent most of his professional career with Brokaw, and his goal had always been to achieve the lowest possible cost by sending out the smallest number of trucks, each carrying the biggest possible load. "The shipping guys couldn't understand how we were going to afford five trucks a week into a market when, at the time, we were only doing two," Radt said. "The idea of using overnight couriers was anathema to them. But we had to do whatever it took to keep our next-day promise. We had to show our customers that we meant what we said. To do that, we had to accept the higher shipping costs, at least initially."

Radt had meeting after meeting with the logistics director. He would agree to the new strategy and try to adhere to it. But, almost as soon as the Minneapolis trial had begun, he reverted to his old ways. He'd refuse to release a half-loaded truck. He'd nix a FedEx shipment. The customer would fail to receive their order. Finally, after making his best effort to get the director on board, Radt gave up and moved him out of logistics and into a different area.

The sales force was slow to embrace the strategy, too. They did not relish the idea of abandoning the exclusive relationships with the big merchants that they had worked so hard to build and maintain. "Some of the sales guys had been playing golf with their customers for twenty years," said Radt. "Now they had to say, 'By the way, starting tomorrow we're going to be selling the same line to three of your biggest competitors.'" It would be even worse calling on prospects, because these would be the accounts the sales force had been ignoring for years. Radt spent hours with the director of sales and his team, lecturing and threatening, and they kept resisting. In the end he had to order them to make the calls. He acknowledged that there were risks involved—they might lose some accounts—but they had no alternative.

The salespeople were right. The process wasn't easy and didn't go smoothly. "Some of the existing customers hated it," said Radt. "One merchant threatened us. 'You do this,' he said, 'and we won't buy another damn thing from you.' The prospects were lukewarm at first. They said, 'We might give it a try, but don't expect any big orders from us.'"

The Minneapolis trial proved that Brokaw really could supply 235 product variations and really could turn around an order for standard product in one day and for custom product in two weeks, and sometimes less. "We were so easy to deal with," says Radt, "that we pleased our existing customers and the new ones started shunting more orders to us. They knew we had trucks going out every day and they'd call and say, 'Can you just throw this or that on for us?' And we'd say yes."

Gradually, the merchants came to realize that one-day delivery could be more than just a convenience to them; it could have an important positive impact on their businesses. The merchant wouldn't need to plan his ordering so far in advance. He wouldn't need to keep as much stock on hand. He would turn his inventory faster, and have less investment tied up in paper stock sitting on the shelf. The Brokaw salesmen gradually learned how to make their case. They told their customers to plan for fifteen inventory turns per year and that they could do even better by reordering frequently.

The Minneapolis trial ran for about ten months, and in each month, Brokaw gained share in that market. Radt decided that the organization was ready to offer the improved service systemwide. He was convinced that the production people had mastered the new control systems and could do the changeovers quickly and with minimal waste. They had confidence that their trucks could deliver into key markets at least once per day. The trial had demonstrated that they could achieve an order fill rate of 96 percent or better. They knew they could turn around a great variety of specialty orders within the two-week delivery window. At that point, the sales force announced to their customers in other Midwestern markets that the new strategy they had told them about was now available.

The results were phenomenal. Demand surged. In key markets, Brokaw's share more than doubled in twenty-four months. Their volume of specialty products increased, as they had hoped and expected it would. But—and this surprised everybody—Brokaw did not lose volume on standard product sales as it had anticipated. Distributors continued to order standard product from Brokaw, despite the 10 percent premium, because of the service advantage.

THE ADVANTAGES OF THE INDIRECT ATTACK

What made Brokaw's indirect attack so successful was the element of surprise. Although Brokaw revealed its new service concept to customers and prospects well before it was launched, the division did not reveal the whole story. Radt and his team did not want a competitor to adopt a similar strategy. They especially did not want a competitor to beat them to it, stealing their advantage.

When Brokaw's executives were asked about their new strategy, they would say that, to offer faster delivery, they would be holding larger inventories of finished goods and working longer hours. Both of these statements were true. But the executives did not mention the new technologies and equipment, new order-management process, and new nonexclusive relationships with customers. They hoped that the competitors, on reading the story, would scoff at Brokaw's efforts or, even better, copy them by increasing inventories and working longer hours. Such changes, made in isolation, would likely raise the competitor's costs and degrade their service.

When the new strategy started to show signs of success, not only were Wausau's competitors surprised, its own employees were amazed, too. Brokaw could barely keep up with demand; in fact, it was constrained by capacity. The demand for specialty product had risen sharply, creating lots of new business.

Wausau's strategy was particularly effective because it did not imperil its competitors. Brokaw focused on the specialty business that their competitors disliked, and did not try to compete head-on in standard product. As a result, the big competitors were content to let Brokaw take the troublesome special orders off their hands and put all their energy into filling the big, standard product orders. Brokaw did not seem to steal volume or profits from them. Although Brokaw did see an increase in demand for standard product, it often purchased it in uncut form from its competitors and finished and repacked it as its own. Thus the competitors were getting a piece of the action even of Brokaw's increased standard business. In effect, Brokaw had created a whole new business. Everyone was happy.

Brokaw's competitors did not counterattack. They remained committed to their fast machines and high-volume business model. They couldn't get their minds around the idea of next-day delivery and product variety. As a result, Brokaw developed decisive advantage by offering a service standard that the others couldn't equal, let alone exceed. Its competitors continued to operate as they had for years, competing on cost and building customer relationships on the golf course.

As its share and profits grew, Brokaw eventually discovered some limitations in the service strategy. There were logistics constraints— it found they could not guarantee next day delivery in all geographies. After a few years, it was producing to capacity and was consistently profitable, but its growth slowed. In order to keep the stock price on the rise, and to keep Brokaw's employees from growing complacent, Dick Radt and his team began to look for new ways to grow. They decided that additional organic growth did not make sense at that time and chose instead to grow through acquisition. In 1993, they purchased the Groveton Mill, in Groveton, New Hampshire, so they could expand Wausau's offering into New England.

WHERE AND HOW TO LOOK FOR ANOMALIES

Brokaw's growth strategy was based on an insight about their anomalously large market share in Chicago. Such anomalies exist in all businesses, but you are more likely to find them in businesses that are characterized by high complexity—those that have a diverse customer base with many segments, defined by volume, product variety, and customer type. The more diverse your customer base, the more likely it is that the standard process cannot be forced to fit all possibilities and that one or more customers will present an anomaly. The diverse base, however, will also make it more difficult for management to see the anomaly, because so much information is available. There may be many inconsistencies and aberrations, and it will be impossible to investigate all of them. Diversity will be further increased if you have multiple layers of distribution—selling through wholesalers and retailers, chains and independents, online and through catalogs. Multiple levels of distribution increase the number of customers and make it more difficult to identify the nonstandard behaviors that have potential for exploitation.

Mature businesses, complex or not, are also fertile breeding grounds for anomalies. Companies in mature business are often set in their ways, resistant to change, and have become prisoners of existing customer relationships. They have become expert at ignoring or dismissing anomalies and, if they see one, might be unable to exploit it or respond if a competitor did so first.

Sometimes you get lucky and stumble across a useful anomaly, but hardball companies go looking for them in an organized way. This is best accomplished by a team whose task is to look for anomalies, analyze their causes, estimate the profit potential they represent, and come up with recommendations for exploiting them. The team should be composed of people from finance, business development, marketing, sales, and operations. They should be given eight weeks or so to identify two or three interesting anomalies. Their specific tasks include:

- Assess the company's productivity across many parameters, (e.g., sales and margin per employee, territory, account, product, service).
- Investigate the practices and activities of the various players in the business: distributors, sales reps, territories, and service techs.
- Develop histograms (bar graphs showing classes and frequencies) of productivity of revenue, cost, and profit drivers.
- Identify and investigate the outliers, such as the customers who buy or sell a great deal more or less than the average. What is their story?
- Spew out ideas about the strategic opportunities that might be embedded in these anomalies.

Once the scouting team has identified a few anomalies and analyzed them, the next step is to distinguish between those anomalies that signal a potential business opportunity from those that are one-time events or have no potential for wider application. The key is to examine the pattern of unusual performance over time. The customers who consistently buy high volumes or the market that outperforms the average year after year are, by definition, not random. Is there an underlying cause that can be identified and then replicated elsewhere?

Here are a few examples of the types of anomalies that might catch the eye of a scouting team:

- Medeco, a manufacturer of high-security locks, has average sales per household in major Canadian cities that are twice the average of its sales per household in the United States, even though Canadian cities are generally safer than those in the United States. Why? What drives those sales in Canada?

- MEC, a consumer electronics brand, is considered a commodity in Japan, where their products sell at a discount to Sony and Matsushita. In the United States, MEC products sell at a premium through specialty retailers. Why?

- Steetley Industrial Distributors has a branch in Oshawa, Ontario, whose gross margins are the lowest of all Steetley's branches, but the branch's sales per employee and return on investment are the highest. Why?

- Mitsubishi Heavy Industry (MHI) often competes against Combustion Engineering for contracts to design and build steam boilers for electric utilities. MHI's win rate is on the rise. They, unlike all the other competitors in the industry, start the design work before they have even won the contract. Is that why they win so often?

Finally, the team needs to understand the precise mechanisms that animate the anomalies they have identified. Exactly what is causing the unusual pattern of performance? What specific features of the product, or the local environment, or the customer experience or operations are bringing it about? Don't accept the usual, too-easy, off-the-top-of-the-head explanations. It's not enough to know, for example, that a particular customer has been loyal for years; you need to know precisely why. (If Radt had accepted that the Chicago merchants had a special relationship with the Brokaw rep, he would not have discovered the real cause of the sales anomaly.) This requires the analysis of internal data and of customer data as well, and may require field interviews with customers, and with their customers.

It is management's job to drive the process. They must create the forum. They must persist in asking "why?" until they gain genuine insight. Business unit personnel may be closest to the details of the anomaly in question, but they are usually too caught up in the day-to-day demands of their jobs to recognize the strategic significance of unusual patterns and practices. It often takes someone who is one step removed to notice and act on anomalies. It also takes an appreciation of differences, a lively sense of curiosity, and a willingness to play with the taken-for-granted rules of the business.

Once an anomaly with likely potential for building strategic advantage has been identified, the work begins. The anomaly must be thoroughly tested and explored before the strategy can be implemented. You must, to start with, understand the economics of the anomaly; the potential sources of growth and increased profitability need to be made explicit.

Before you exploit the anomaly more widely across your system, it may be necessary to change or improve your business systems. You may also need to adjust or refine your organization structure, in order to remove functional barriers and change dysfunctional behaviors that could blunt or prevent the successful exploitation of the anomaly.

You must consider how your customers and competitors will view your strategy and how they might react. To understand your customers' views, you should test the concept with a subset of customers to prove the viability and value of the strategy.

It will be necessary to prepare a marketing plan. It should include a press and public information strategy that will bring your current customers into the new system by convincing them of its benefits. Your communication activities should keep your competitors guessing or cause them to take inappropriate action and give you as big a lead as possible. Your marketing plan should also include activities that will help you identify and target potential customers, particularly anomalous customers of your competitors.

Anomaly hunting is best done at certain times of the year. The worst time to look for anomalies is during a budget review, when everyone is worried about control numbers. A much better time is in a strategic review, when everyone should be prepared to think creatively about the future. Often, by reflecting on their past—including strategies and business results—companies can find opportunities they can exploit in a systematic way.

WHAT A WINNING ANOMALY LOOKS LIKE

A win is when you can retain and grow the business of your anomalous, highly profitable customers when you implement the new strategy. And, even more delightful, when you can capture the business of your competitors' customers. The majority of Brokaw's growth, for example, came from new merchants, the ones the company had no prior relationship with. Brokaw enticed these merchants with its improved service offering and hooked them with its ability to manage specialty orders. Not only did most of the existing specialty business come Brokaw's way, its skill created incremental business. Such incremental business comes from your competitors' customers and reinforces the basic economics underlying the anomaly. In the case of Brokaw, the more specialty business Brokaw was able to attract through its legacy merchants and its new merchants, the lower was the per customer cost of providing fast service. As more and more of the specialty orders migrated to Brokaw, there was less and less specialty business available to any competitor who might try to challenge the company.

The most successful win is the one that your competitor may not immediately recognize as a win, can't figure out, or may even see as a loss. It took years for Brokaw's competitors to realize that the information they had gotten in the press did not tell the whole story of how Brokaw had achieved its win. Besides, because their own core business was barely affected, they asked themselves, "Why make a move if we don't have to?"

Taking advantage of an anomaly is an opportunity to inject into your company some of the vitality, excitement, and spirit of experimentation that is characteristic of start-ups. Every day, entrepreneurs are working to reinvent your business and carve out a piece of it for themselves. By capitalizing on anomalies, you can harness the same kind of creative energy and put growth back on your company's agenda.

FOUR

Threaten Your Competitor's Profit Sanctuaries

At times, wouldn't you like to influence the behavior of a competitor? Get him to back off and not enter a segment of the market that is attractive to you? Cause him to slow down his investments in product development or production technology in areas that are key to your business?

You can influence the behaviors of a competitor if you can determine where his profit sanctuaries are. Profit sanctuaries are the parts of your competitor's product, service, and geographic portfolio where he makes the most money. Every company has one or more profit sanctuaries, and they are important not only because they deliver healthy profits to the bottom line, but because they usually fund other—weaker or developing—parts of the business.

There are many ways to put pressure on a competitor's profit sanctuaries. You can compete aggressively on price on selected products or in selected geographies where you go head-to-head with your competitor. You can offer products with new features, or special combinations of features, at prices that will suck volume away from its products. You can increase service, while holding prices, on a portion of your offering where your own profitability is fairly minor but that provides a major source of your competitor's profitability.

There are also many things you cannot do when attacking your competitor's profit sanctuaries, because they involve pricing practices that may be seen as anticompetitive and therefore will raise substantial risks of civil and criminal liability. U.S. federal and state laws, as well as the laws of many countries, for example, prohibit predatory pricing, which is generally defined as selling goods or services at an unreasonably low price with the intent of driving a competitor out of business. Other statutes make price discrimination criminal where the effect of such discrimination may be to substantially lessen competition or tend to create a monopoly in any line of commerce. These laws define areas that lie well beyond the caution zone, and leaders must draw a very bright line at a safe distance from them. (Make sure your lawyers know, or learn, the statutes and regulations that apply to your strategy in every area where you intend to pursue it.)

The goal of devastating a competitor's profit sanctuaries is not to force your rival out of business or to create a monopoly within your industry for yourself. Rather, the goal is choke the flow of cash from your competitor's profit sanctuaries, forcing it to change specific actions or behaviors that are detrimental to you. If it doesn't, it risks an incursion into its profit sanctuaries that will, in turn, put pressure on other areas of its business.

JAPANESE AUTOMAKERS ATTACK THE LIGHT TRUCK PROFIT SANCTUARY OF THE BIG THREE

In the early 2000s, the leading Japanese automakers—Toyota, Nissan, and Honda—took aim at an important profit sanctuary of the Big Three North American automakers: light trucks. Their success in the attack will likely determine the futures of General Motors, Ford, and Chrysler.

Until recently, the Japanese automakers have employed a different hardball strategy to build share and grow profits in the American market. They have generally attacked indirectly, introducing products at the low end of the price range, or in the small size segment, and gradually creeping up to higher-priced and larger-sized cars only after building a customer base. They have supported this strategy by consistently offering better-quality vehicles at lower prices than American competitors.

To keep development costs low, they have offered vehicles based on designs created for the Japanese market and modified slightly for American tastes.

This has been the competitive pattern for the past thirty years, and it has taken the form of a series of skirmishes. Each time the Japanese automakers offered a car of higher price or larger size, the Big Three would make noise and then retreat. Sometimes they would seek sanctuary in cease-fire deals, known as "voluntary restraint agreements." More often, they would put their energy into creating new profit sanctuaries in more profitable vehicles, such as luxury cars and minivans and, most important, SUVs and light trucks. There was one main thing that kept the Big Three from completely abandoning the lower-priced vehicle market to the Japanese—they had to meet the U.S. corporate average fuel economy (CAFE) standards. The fuel economy on their larger, more profitable vehicles was so poor they needed their smaller, more fuel-efficient cars in order to reduce the CAFE of the entire line.

The Big Three did not think of their actions as retreats, of course, but rather as product innovation and a shift of product mix to meet customer demand. For a while, profits rose at General Motors, Ford, and Chrysler, with the majority of profits from auto-manufacturing operations (as opposed to finance and other nonauto operations) coming from the new sanctuaries: minivans, SUVs, and pick-ups. By the late 1990s, the Big Three sold more light trucks in North America than they did cars, and they were thankful for this. After all, the Ford Expedition and GM Suburban could bring in $10,000 or more in profit for each vehicle sold. But by 2001, the profit decline of the Big Three's faltering car businesses became a drag on the profitability of their light truck businesses. In that year, Ford made a substantial profit from its light truck business, but the profit was almost wiped out by big losses on cars.

As the Big Three were shifting volume to light trucks, the Japanese were changing their competitive focus. By the end of the 1990s, they offered a full line of cars, from small to large in size, from low to high in price; they offered compact trucks, and mini-minivans, and small SUVs. But they did not offer a full-size light truck with the heft and power that American consumers so dearly love.

So, the Japanese automakers decided to introduce new styles especially for the North American market—including full-size minivans,

SUVS, and heftier light trucks. At first, the Big Three seemed not to worry and the media paid little attention. The truck was seen as a quintessentially American phenomenon that could never be threatened by a foreign intruder. Didn't American consumers expect their trucks to be made by the Big Three and only by the Big Three? The Ford F150, Chevy Silverado 2500, and Dodge Ram were not only best sellers, after all—they were American icons.

The initial attempts of the Japanese to move up from compact trucks to full-size trucks were only modest successes. The Toyota Tundra was derided by some members of the press as not being as tough as the Big Three trucks. It does not matter that more than half of the buyers of light trucks use their vehicles to commute to work and to haul the occasional sheet of plywood on weekends. They don't need and never use the full gross weight of their vehicle, but they still want it.

Gradually, North American consumers accepted the Japanese light truck offerings, just as they had their cars, and the Japanese automakers steadily grew their share of the market. From 1980 to 1995, the major Japanese light truck manufacturers had a nearly constant share of 10 percent. The North American producers held the rest of the share. By early 2000, the Japanese leaders had grown their share to almost 25 percent and Detroit's share had fallen to 75 percent.

The Japanese onslaught into light trucks will continue. The Japanese automakers have been able to hold their prices, helped by the higher resale value their vehicles command thanks to their better quality. In late 2003, Nissan introduced the Titan, designed to challenge Ford's F150, and Toyota announced that it might compete in heavier trucks, setting its sights on the Ford F250 and the GM Silverado, vehicles that can deliver as much as $15,000 profit per vehicle to their makers. At the 2004 Detroit Auto Show, Toyota, Nissan, and Honda took center stage with their new, brutish pick-ups. Where were GM, Ford, and Chrysler? Ford, at least, showed signs of fighting back to regain share in its core car segment. Ford declared 2004 to be the "Year of the Car" and announced plans to introduce as many as six new car models, including the Ford 500. Is this a direct attack on Toyota's profit sanctuary—cars made for the U.S. market—where the Japanese company makes about 70 percent of its profit from operations?

Meanwhile, the Japanese automakers continue to play hardball, working diligently to threaten the Big Three's richest remaining profit sanctuary. This is a terrible situation for any company to be in. Despite Ford's aggressive program of new models, it is a long shot that their quality, styling, and price will be good enough to gain significant car share against the Japanese.

This is a straightforward example of an entire class of competitors, the Japanese automakers, attacking the profit sanctuaries of established leaders. The result is that Toyota, Nissan, and Honda now indirectly control the cash faucets of GM, Ford, and Chrysler. For some time to come, the strategies of the Big Three will be what Toyota allows them be.

Toyota says it will achieve a 15 percent share of the worldwide automotive market. Devastating the profit sanctuaries of its main rivals is one way to reduce the effort required to get there.

VACUCORP WARNS SWEEPCO AWAY FROM ITS PROFIT SANCTUARY

Another reason for attacking a competitor's profit sanctuary is to make it difficult for a competitor to make a certain move or to put pressure on one of its current activities. Such an attack can cause a competitor to reconsider its actions and modify its behavior in ways that suit the attacker.

A strategy to threaten a competitor's profit sanctuary usually requires approaching the caution zone. As we've said already, and as our legal advisors wish us to make more than abundantly clear, attacking a profit sanctuary may involve the use of pricing tactics that can put you at risk of being charged with anticompetitive activity. Consequently, even companies that employ this strategy completely legally are rarely, if ever, willing to reveal what they are doing while they're doing it, or discuss in detail what they did after the fact. As a result, we have translated the following story from one industry (which shall remain unidentified) to another, household appliances, in order to disguise the identity of the companies involved.[1]

The worldwide demand for vacuum cleaners is over $1 billion in sales and growing at about 4 percent per year. In North America the market is about $700 billion, growing at 3 percent annually, and there are three major, full-line companies. Of these, VacuCorp is the leader, offering a full range of vacuum cleaning products, from portables to built-in vacuum cleaning systems. It is also the world leader in the design, manufacture, and marketing of general household appliances. There are also a handful of companies in the industry with narrow offerings that, although hanging on by their fingernails, can cause a great deal of disruption to the industry. SweepCo is one of them.

All the competitors in vacuum cleaners have a base business, offering standard products to a set of regular accounts, with well-established profit sanctuaries. VacuCorp's profit sanctuary is upright vacuum cleaners sold to national retail accounts. Competition in the industry generally occurs at the margins, usually when a major account—such as a big retailer, wholesaler, or homebuilder—decides to put its business in review and opens it up for competitive bids. When this happens, a company like SweepCo has almost nothing to lose by lowballing its bid, with the hope of adding its line of products to the retailer's mix. The incremental sales and profit can be attractive to it, and will bleed profitability out of the account for VacuCorp.

This tactic became an increasingly nettlesome problem for VacuCorp. SweepCo was staying in business by buying incremental volume for itself with its low-margin, sometimes break-even, bids. As a result, several accounts that had long been cozy profit sanctuaries for VacuCorp were gradually losing their warmth.

What could VacuCorp do? How could it get SweepCo to rein in its aggressive behavior?

VacuCorp set out to understand SweepCo's business model. Why would a company so doggedly go after incremental, low-margin sales? Usually, such companies have low fixed costs. In SweepCo's case, they had low capital costs, with little debt and fully depreciated assets. Their major cost was in labor—nonunionized and much of it part-time—which they could adjust to fit production volume. When they won incremental business, they could quickly hire more people to build the product. When they lost incremental business, they quickly laid off people before the cash drain hit. This made it possible for SweepCo to keep going after low-margin business, constantly adjusting its workforce to keep profits just slightly ahead of costs.

But SweepCo could not survive on that business alone. The Vacu-Corp management guessed that SweepCo must have a profit sanctuary, a highly-profitable business that kept it going through the ups and downs of pursuing incremental sales. To find it, VacuCorp did a competitive teardown of SweepCo. It compared and contrasted itself with its smaller rival along many dimensions including:

- Product offerings
- Technologies and designs
- Geographic and account strength and weaknesses
- Pricing and history
- Manufacturing, supplier, and distribution footprint
- Cost estimates, reached by estimating product volume per account, and per factory

Based on this analysis, VacuCorp guessed that a big proportion of SweepCo's profits came from a single product—a canister vacuum cleaner, made in a single plant in Iowa. The canister vacuum cleaner sits on four wheels like a metal kitchen trash can on its side, with a hose and cord brilliantly designed to tangle themselves around furniture and the user's legs. The canister was all the rage in the 1960s, but lost its appeal when portables and lightweight uprights were introduced and became increasingly popular. Sales of canisters dropped dramatically but then stabilized at a low level. The big producers dumped their canister lines, leaving just enough business to support a few small manufacturers, one of which was SweepCo. The company made a lot of money, indeed the great majority of its money, on the Iowa-made canister vacuum cleaner.

The management of VacuCorp decided they might be able to encourage SweepCo to stop making its lowball bids on VacuCorp's national accounts by attacking SweepCo's canister business with a new canister product of their own. VacuCorp believed it could produce a canister at lower cost than SweepCo, by reducing the number of parts per machine in comparison to the SweepCo models. It could also make the model more appealing to consumers by using more plastic components to reduce the product weight, installing more efficient and powerful motors that would improve performance, and incorporating electronic controls that were cheaper to produce and also provided features the SweepCo model couldn't match. The new VacuCorp canister would be smaller, more attractive, easier to use, and cheaper to buy than the SweepCo. The product would be produced at an existing plant that had plenty of surplus capacity, so VacuCorp could supply all the volume it needed with little additional overhead. VacuCorp's costs would be so low that the company would have tremendous flexibility in pricing and could significantly undercut SweepCo's prices.

VacuCorp did not care about the canister business at all. It planned to use the new canister to attack SweepCo only when the rival showed up to make a lowball bid on one of VacuCorp's national accounts. It would introduce the canister at a price lower than that of SweepCo's product (although above its own cost) and was prepared to drop the price even lower if necessary (but still above cost).

VacuCorp began production of the new product and steadily built inventory. The first time SweepCo made a move on one of VacuCorp's national accounts with a lowball bid on uprights, VacuCorp was knocking on the door of one of SweepCo's major canister accounts within a few days. With its new product's advanced features and lower price, VacuCorp won the sale and displaced SweepCo. And so it went. After several such skirmishes, SweepCo got the indirect message: "Keep away from our key accounts. If you come after us, we'll retaliate. We'll undercut your prices and cut off your cash flow." The prospect of losing its canister business, which delivered more than two-thirds of its total profits, was too painful to endure. Within a few months, SweepCo rarely attacked a VacuCorp national account. And VacuCorp was able to scale back production of the canister product, keeping only enough inventory to beat back the occasional, ill-advised SweepCo raid.

Peace settled over the vacuum cleaner industry.

MAKING A SUCCESS OF HARDBALL PRICING

In both these cases, management chose to attack their competitor's profit sanctuary to achieve a specific business objective. The Japanese automakers sought to steal market share from the Big Three. VacuCorp sought to protect its own profit sanctuary from the debilitating raids of its competitor. For both, management used sophisticated insight and business intelligence to make bold and effective attacks. They did so not to be vandals or bullies, not to destroy their competitors or achieve market domination, but to influence and alter the behaviors of their competitors in specific ways relative to specific markets and products.

A key weapon in both cases was pricing—hardball competitors often set their prices to respond to competitive circumstances and influence their competitor's behaviors. Strategic pricing to threaten profit sanctuaries works best to meet the following objectives:

- When you want to grow an area of your business but are concerned about the amount of resources your competitor may have to use against you. In this case, you want to price strategically to sharply diminish a competitor's cash flow, thereby reducing his ability to respond.

- When a competitor is making a move into an area of your business—product, service, or geography—that has traditionally been your stronghold and you want him to stop or slow down. With strategic pricing, you can put pressure on the competitor's cash flow where he least expects or wants it. This is what VacuCorp did.

You have the best chance of achieving these objectives when certain market conditions exist:

- *Competition is strongly based on price.* When this is the case, even a small move in price—up or down—will quickly cause a shift in sales volume. The more like a commodity the product or service is, the easier it will be to use price to attract customers away from a competitor. In air travel, for example, the service is a commodity and switching costs are low. One carrier can grab traffic from another by slicing the price of the fare. The higher the costs of switching, however, the harder it will be to lure customers away with price.

- *Customers are concentrated in the category.* If your customer base is highly fragmented, influencing a competitor through a strategic price cut is very hard. Prices have to be cut for a lot of customers before any real influence over a competitor is achieved. When the customer base is concentrated, such as is the case with big box retailers, discounts can be used to set low prices for high-volume customers.

- *The competitors have broad product or service offerings and a large geographic presence.* Such complexity often means that the competitive positions in specific categories or geographies will vary dramatically. In one product, competitor A may be the market leader with product X in geography Z, while competitor B may lead geography Z with product M. The more complex the businesses and variable the positions are, the more difficult it is for management to analyze one another's business. But the complexity also gives management greater freedom to make focused pricing moves on specific products, accounts, or geographies. You must be sure that your "costs to serve" and specific market and competitive conditions are well-documented in case you have to defend yourself against charges of predatory pricing.

- *Your product and service offerings, and your geographic markets, do not overlap completely with those of your competitor, or, if they do, only in a very limited way.* You need to have sanctuaries of your own as well as targets. When the Japanese—especially Toyota and Nissan—came to America, their profit sanctuary was their passenger vehicle business in Japan. But the Big Three had virtually no base in Japan from which they could attack this profit sanctuary. For the Big Three, all fights had to be conducted on home soil.

- *There is overlap and the competitor has the leading market share and can be made to suffer great pain with very little effort from you.* Imagine if the situation in appliances had been reversed, for example, and it was SweepCo that sought a change in behavior from VacuCorp. SweepCo was in a perfect position to drop its prices to key VacuCorp accounts. With very little share in these accounts, the drop in price would have had a minimal effect on SweepCo. But VacuCorp would have been forced to drop its price to meet SweepCo's challenge, and would instantly have felt the pain. A small reduction in profitability for SweepCo would result in a big reduction for VacuCorp.

It's easier to influence the behavior of your competitors when you have a good understanding of how they actually behave. If your competitor is generally aware and a fast responder, you may be able to send it a signal (as VacuCorp did by bidding on a few accounts, as a warning) and quickly achieve the desired effect. If the competitor is a slow responder, you may need to choke off the cash flow from a profit sanctuary before it gets the message. Behaviors to look for include:

- The company has only average financial performance or, better yet, poor financial results. It will not have the resources to resist a strategic pricing attack even if it has the will and intelligence to do so. It is likely to hear the message quickly and make the desired changes to reduce the heat.

- The competitor is sluggish, unaware, or does not display aggressive tendencies. Many businesses are followers; their management teams simply do what other companies do. Many more are clueless. You can attack the profit sanctuaries of follower or clueless businesses and it can take months for them to notice, more months to come up with a response, and even more months to execute it. By the time they are ready to make an offensive move, the damage has been done and they are sent reeling. Usually, these are well-known, characteristic behaviors and are easy to identify. It was no secret, for example, that the Big Three automakers were unresponsive companies.

- Its business units are managed as independent profit centers. The flow of information will be slow. It will take your competitor more time to realize an attack is under way than if it were organized as a single profit center. The response will take longer to organize and execute.

- It has a weak corporate center. A weak central management team will do nothing to help a business unit whose profit sanctuary is under attack, but they will still expect the unit to continue delivering profit against target. This is an impossible mission. The leaders of the unit will be forced to make up their own counterattacks (usually without sufficient resources), or to give up in frustration, causing a talent drain. Competitors that are owned by weak corporate centers will often "sell themselves down the river" to survive the short term.

SOURCES OF INSIGHT AND A WORD OF CAUTION

When a management team is considering the use of pricing to influence a competitor's behavior, it must be sure to gain sufficient information and insight to ensure that the attack will work, achieve the desired result, and not backfire. The following knowledge must be gathered before launching an attack:

- Your own costs, prices, and profitability by category, geography, and account.

- Customer concentration by product, category, and geography.

- Your competitor's history of pricing variations, category offerings, account management, and shifts in geographic focus.

- Extensive and deep competitive cost benchmarking of products within the category, the supply base, and the costs to serve the market. The latter costs—of getting a product or service into the hands of a customer and getting paid—can be substantial, not always easy to see or estimate, and may vary dramatically by customer. In parcel delivery, for example, it costs less to serve a customer that sends or receives many packages a day than a customer that sends one or two a week. A competitor with a large share of high-volume customers will usually make a higher profit per package, even if it offers a volume discount, because its cost per parcel is lower than it would be if the company serviced many small volume customers. Thus a profit sanctuary is created.

- Your competitors' organization, management team profile, standard practices, and performance.

- The financial strength of all the major competitors, the sources of their funds, and how they use them.

This knowledge will enable you to game your competitor's response, whatever it may be, to advance your strategy for devastating their profit sanctuary. You will know how much you can and should use price as a persuader. You'll have identified what the early warning signs of failure or success are likely to be. You'll have guessed how the competitor might respond if it doesn't retreat.

These insights will allow you to better orchestrate your attack. You may choose to hold prices down until the competitor clearly demonstrates that he has gotten the message and starts to change his behavior. Or you may want to drop prices sharply and then unexpectedly raise them so as to punch the buttons of your competitor's management team and throw them off balance. To really get their heads spinning, you can make sharp pricing moves in different directions in different categories in different geographies—all at once or at different times. The competitor will be forced to spend a great deal of time gathering information, trying to analyze it, and developing a response. By the time it has done so, your pricing will have changed again.

There are risks in using pricing to threaten a competitor's profit sanctuary. These include:

- The competitor may not be clueless at all and may have good knowledge about your business. It may quickly see your strategy and be able to attack your profit sanctuaries in return. It may be able to use pricing in retaliation and send your team into confusion. This should not happen if you have properly prepared. But, if the possibility exists, you might want to consider a different strategy.

- The competitor may have greater financial strength than you had estimated, such as off-balance sheet resources that give it greater ability to withstand an attack, wait out a raid, and commit resources to a powerful response. Again, good preparation is paramount.

- A sugar daddy could show up unexpectedly. Whoops. If Mr. Big Bucks arrives to save the day, be sure you have an exit strategy ready.

- Your competitor may be willing to contest your actions on legal grounds, even if you have done nothing wrong. Because what constitutes "anti-competitive" activity is open to interpretation, you may find yourself devoting more management time and more money for legal fees than you had planned, or would like.

The use of hardball pricing to threaten a competitor's profit sanctuary and get him to change a behavior sounds straightforward. But executing it with minimal mistakes and maximum results is difficult. Insight and good planning are key. The management team must be willing to take risks and have the courage to press the attack even when the going gets rough. And it is essential that you have good legal counsel throughout the process of planning and executing your strategy.

An attack on a profit sanctuary, especially through pricing, will very likely cause a fierce competitive reaction. It should not be undertaken by the faint of heart.

FIVE

Take It and
Make It Your Own

Not every hardball strategy requires great originality of thought or the creation of something brand new. Many businesses achieve success by recognizing the value of an existing idea, practice, or business model and making it their own.

Ray Kroc didn't invent the fast food restaurant or the assembly line burger. He recognized the potential of Dick and Mac McDonald's Southern California burger joint, cut a deal to franchise it, built the McDonald's Corporation, and eventually bought out the founding brothers. (Kroc first spotted the business as an anomaly—he was the exclusive distributor of a milkshake machine called the Multimixer and was amazed when he learned that the McDonald's restaurant had ordered eight of them.) Similarly, The Home Depot founders Arthur Blank and Bernie Marcus didn't invent the first warehouse hardware chain. They borrowed the big box concept from their earlier employer, Handy Dan, evolved it into an even bigger box and expanded it throughout North America.

Hardball players are not victims of the NIH (not invented here) syndrome. They are always on the lookout for ideas they can adopt or adapt. They look at competitors in their own industry for trade practices, pricing schemes, product designs, technologies, employee hiring and development methods, approaches to supplier management, and customer focus tactics that are better than their own. They also look in other industries for innovations—such as time and quality management methods, alternative channels, and supply chain management tactics—that have not yet appeared in their own.

But hardball players are not copycats. They are not plagiarists or knock-off artists. They don't infringe on copyrights or steal patents. When they identify a good idea, they find a way to improve it. The founder of Kmart claimed that Sam Walton, founder of Wal-Mart, "not only copied our concepts, he strengthened them. Sam took the ball and ran with it."[1]

Hardball players know that good, proven ideas are hard to come by and are not shy about taking them for their own. In so doing, the hardball company is often able to create a competitive advantage, often faster than it would otherwise, and sometimes even decisive advantage.

PUTTING NEW LIFE INTO THE CASKET BUSINESS

The Batesville Casket Company (BCC), based in Batesville, Indiana, found a way to gain competitive advantage, grow, and become the world's largest designer, marketer, manufacturer, and distributor of burial caskets by adapting the standards and procedures of Japanese car makers.

In the late 1980s, Batesville Casket, a division of Hillenbrand Industries, was a successful maker of steel and wood caskets. But its performance was flattening and it, like the entire industry, was virtually innovation-free. Hillenbrand wanted growth from Batesville, as it did from all its subsidiaries, and brought in a new executive, Bob Irwin, to get it.

Irwin had spent his career in the automotive industry, much of it as head of manufacturing for the Australian operations of Chrysler. When Chrysler came to the brink of financial disaster in the early 1980s, it sold its Australian operations to Mitsubishi Motors Corporation (MMC). Almost immediately, Mitsubishi sent in a team of engineers to convert the manufacturing process to its version of the Toyota Production System (TPS). Within a year, the organization had cut inventories throughout the plant, raised quality, lowered costs, and created a culture of continuous improvement. Bob Irwin was part of the effort, and he learned well.

Although he knew little about the burial casket industry, Irwin found much that he was familiar with when he arrived at Batesville. Like the auto-making process, the traditional casket-making process begins with sheets of steel. The sheets are cut to shape and then formed by large presses into the major components. The parts are then welded together, some by hand and some by automated equipment, to form the casket shell. The welds are ground and polished. The shells are painted in automated booths and sent to assembly, where the interiors and trim are installed, and the finished caskets are then released to shipping. Production is done in large batches, and the manufacturing floor is organized around machine type, material lots, and storage for components and semi-finished assemblies.

Like the U.S. auto industry in the 1980s, the casket industry also had a quality problem. Exterior components were often scratched or dented, and the interior finishing damaged or soiled, either in the manufacturing process or during shipment to the distribution centers and funeral homes. The high incidence of defects meant that the manufacturing plant had to include many steps for rework and repair. Batesville's distribution centers also had repair facilities.

To Bob Irwin, this looked depressingly familiar, reminding him of the seemingly endless cycle of rework that had become standard procedure at Chrysler Australia before MMC arrived on the scene. Irwin knew that if Batesville could eliminate the tremendous waste in the manufacturing process it could dramatically lower costs. This would enable the company to offer customers higher-quality products than their competitors did, and even to lower their prices. They might then be able to build volume and increase the bottom line, as well. If so, they could invest their earnings in product innovations that would further build volume and profits. Competitive advantage gained by manufacturing process improvement might lead to decisive advantage.[2]

Batesville already had experience in adopting manufacturing practices from the automotive industry. In the late 1970s, it had moved from one-off, hand assembly to a large-batch, automated assembly line similar to that employed by the American automakers. Now Irwin was asking the company to make another major capital investment in equipment and systems, plant reorganization, and employee education. The investment was large enough that it could place a tremendous strain on Batesville's financial resources and amounted to a bet-the-company move. But as far as he could tell, there was no competitor contemplating any such dramatic moves or, for that matter, any moves at all.

Irwin began by focusing on quality. He wanted to achieve a zero defects standard throughout the process and eliminate all repair work. First, he shut down the repair functions in the distribution centers, because he wanted to keep all the improvement efforts in one place, the manufacturing plant. So, if a casket arrived at a distribution center in a damaged condition, it had to be returned to the factory for repair. If it was damaged during handling at the distribution center, it also had to be returned to the factory. The distribution center and manufacturing staff were charged with identifying the cause of the damage and eliminating it. To underline the importance of the effort, and make it a blatant part of management's day, Irwin had several of the defective caskets placed on display in Batesville's executive offices. It was the job of the management team to determine the causes of the dents and bruises, tears and scratches, and get rid of them.

Irwin worked with his production team to revamp Batesville's manufacturing operations, installing a casket-making version of TPS. The production process was streamlined, in-process storage was reduced, and the number of steps needed to handle materials was cut back. Batesville was able to shorten set-up times, especially for the big stamping machines. It installed more automated equipment, which significantly improved yield and lowered defect rates, particularly in welding. Automation also enabled the company to reduce its reliance on manual labor for operations, such as materials handling, that did not add customer value. With greater speed and higher-quality, Batesville was able to reduce its batch sizes, which meant it could produce a greater variety of products and shorten order turnaround. Not only did quality improve, productivity did, too.

Next, Irwin took on the supply chain. He began by analyzing the relationship between Batesville and its suppliers. In the auto industry, the manufacturer usually pays its suppliers long after the parts it delivers are actually used. In Japan, for example, automakers typically use a supplier's parts within a few days of delivery but may take as long as 180 days to pay. Batesville, Indiana, is not Japan. In Batesville, suppliers' invoices were marked "Net 30." In practice, that meant the check usually arrived within forty-five working days after delivery. Irwin offered to pay the suppliers within a week of the time their material was used. In return for speedy payment, Irwin asked the suppliers to own and manage their inventories of raw material within the Batesville factory. Both the supplier and BCC would sign off on the accuracy of the bill of material. When manufacturing pulled a part from inventory, accounts payable would be instructed to send payment.

Irwin also looked at BCC's distribution practices to see how they matched the needs of its customers. Funeral directors do not maintain big inventories because caskets are too large to store and too expensive to carry on the books. Standard practice is for the funeral director to order a casket as soon the customer has made his choice and then set the date for the funeral, or viewing of the deceased, within a few days of placing the order. (The funeral director has no choice but to use the actual casket the customer has ordered for the viewing because it is illegal to reuse a casket.) Irwin found that funeral directors were caught in a compromise. They had been forced to settle for slow delivery and had come to believe that faster delivery from the big suppliers was impossible. What they really wanted, of course, was next-day delivery. They could only dream of same-day delivery.

Although Batesville's revamped manufacturing process would be able to meet the needs of the funeral directors, the distribution network would not. It had been designed and optimized not for quality, speed, or variety, but for lowest possible cost. Batesville maintained a number of regional distribution centers, most of them located on the outskirts of large metropolitan areas. As the caskets were built they would be held at the factory until there were enough to fill a truck to be dispatched to a distribution center. The caskets were held at the distribution center and, when an order came in, delivered to the funeral home by a small truck.

The effect of this distribution process was that funeral home directors could not be assured of next-day delivery, except if a casket was in stock at the distribution center and a truck happened to be leaving the center that day with space for another order. Sometimes the funeral director would have to wait several days for the casket to be shipped from the factory to the distribution center, or for the distribution center to put together enough orders to fill a truck. The wait put the funeral director in an awkward situation with the family of the deceased.

Bill Irwin asked his team to review the distribution network to see how it might be improved. Perhaps they could site the distribution centers closer to central business districts. Maybe they could run a larger fleet of smaller route trucks. The team concluded they could do a number of things to enhance delivery, but that it would increase costs.

To justify the additional cost, Irwin believed that it would be necessary to increase the volume of Batesville's business, so he looked for opportunities to increase the top line. Although Batesville was already the largest volume producer of steel and wood caskets in the United States and Canada, there were still many local casket producers in major metro areas, and they did a substantial volume of business. Their competitive advantage was the ability to customize caskets and deliver them quickly, sometimes the next day, to local funeral homes. Irwin and his team decided that, if they could combine customization with high-quality and speedy delivery, they could capture business from the local producers. Irwin again borrowed from his experience with car making to adapt the manufacturing process so Batesville could efficiently build and finish a much larger number of product variations.

Bill Irwin did not have an easy job adapting the practices of the Japanese auto industry. Many of his management team members, and most of the organization at large, found it difficult to give up long-standing practices. But Irwin was a hardball manager who took a hardball approach to planning, promoting, and executing change. He often spoke in ultimatums that became known around the plant as Irwin-isms. "It's my way or the highway," he would say when he encountered resistance from his team or manufacturing staff, or, "Do it, or you're done." He admitted that he was tough and relentless. "I used the Chinese water torture method," he said. "I never let up on my demands. Drip, drip, drip, and change happened."

Despite his tough manner, people in the organization could see that Irwin was committed and personally involved. He was a visible presence in Batesville's hallways, factories, and distribution centers. He stuck with his program and it led to tangible results. Under his watch, Batesville improved manufacturing quality, reduced costs, sped up distribution, and increased product variety, all of which enabled it to better meet the needs of their customers, which led to increased volume and market share. Its competitors could not match Batesville's production or distribution systems and, as Batesville's volume grew, no competitor had enough business to generate the resources to try.

The automotive manufacturing model was available to any casket producer to copy, but only Bill Irwin was willing to be a hardball adapter. The result: Batesville resembles its model, Toyota, with a process competitors can't beat and a market share they are unable to steal.

FORD CUSTOMER SERVICE DIVISION: FINDING THE RIGHT MODEL TO COPY

It is not always obvious which model is the best one to copy. Ford Customer Service Division (FCSD) failed at several attempts at capitalizing on a competitor's success before they got it right.[3]

In the early 1990s, Ford's service division—which supplies the aftermarket parts and service techniques to repair Ford vehicles in the Ford dealerships—had stalled. Revenues were flat. Of Ford's five thousand dealerships, only a few hundred were achieving revenue growth from their service operations. In most capital goods industries, aftermarket operations grow faster than the original equipment operations. But at Ford, customer service was growing more slowly than the original equipment business. Something was wrong with this picture.

FCSD fiddled with several strategies to stimulate growth. At the time, quality was the popular industrial mantra, and a focus on quality had worked wonders on the Ford assembly line. FCSD decided to recite the mantra themselves, and developed a quality program called "Fix It Right First Time." The goal was 100 percent service satisfaction. It sounded good, but it wasn't. Implementation was impossible. Most of the repair problems were the result of design or manufacturing flaws and they couldn't be fixed at the dealership. The "Fix It Right First Time" program disappointed customers, frustrated service technicians, and had no positive effect on revenue. Ford let the program slowly wither.

Next, FCSD looked to its competitors for inspiration. They saw that many retail service providers, such as Jiffy Lube, Midas, Pep Boys, and others, were enjoying a brisk business. Ford considered the idea of creating its own stand-alone service operation that would be called Ford Auto Care. By taking the service operation out of the dealership, where service was an also-ran in comparison to auto sales, it might be able to leverage the Ford brand name in a related service business. GE had done it with equipment leasing and insurance. GM had done it with finance. Why couldn't Ford do it with auto service? In the end, Ford's dealers, a powerful group within the Ford empire, nixed the idea. They couldn't agree where the service shops should be located and worried that their own service operations would be cannibalized.

In frustration, Ford's senior leadership selected a group of talented executives, dubbed them the growth team, and charged them with finding ways to grow the service business, fast. The Ford team did what borrowers should always do first: their homework. They gathered information about the market, compared themselves to their competitors, sized the opportunity, identified successful practices, and considered strategies for achieving growth and building share.

The team first delved into their existing customer database, which contained extensive information collected from thousands of surveys and other customer response mechanisms. The team analyzed the data, trying to understand how Ford's service operations worked and how they didn't. They analyzed customers by demographics and service records. They looked at statistics by dealer, by brand and model, and by competitor. They studied a wealth of data for both new and used vehicles, about most common repairs and service intervals. They also looked at manufacturing data, including volumes, defect and rework levels, supplier quality, and warranty repairs.

After all this data mining, the team focused on one important indicator—the percentage of customers who serviced their Ford vehicles at the Ford dealership where they had bought their cars. What they found was alarming. In the first year of ownership, Ford owners brought their cars to the Ford dealership for less than half of the maintenance or repair jobs they needed done. For more than half of the service jobs, however, customers apparently felt that the Ford dealership offered no special service benefit, and took their cars to a retail service chain or a local garage. In the second year of ownership, and thereafter, customers returned to the Ford dealership even less often when they needed service.

The growth team was surprised by this lack of customer loyalty to their dealerships, but they were shocked when they saw the numbers for some of their competitors. Honda had much better scores than Ford. During the first year of ownership, Honda owners brought their vehicles to the Honda dealership for 70 percent of their service needs. (Saturn, by the way, was in a class by itself and scored even higher than Honda. However, Saturn had a total dealership experience that FCSD could not hope to replicate, and so they set their sights on Honda.)

The growth team was further convinced that Honda was the best model to follow by another piece of data they discovered. After the first year, the rate of decline in customer loyalty was the same for Honda as it was for Ford. Theoretically, then, if Ford could crank up their initial loyalty rate close to Honda's, they would keep higher levels of service business throughout the life of the relationship with the customer. Based on this insight, the growth team calculated they could grow Ford's service business by more than 50 percent.

Next question: How could Ford match Honda's service excellence? It was time to get to the rock face and take a good look.

The team visited dozens of dealerships. They found that Honda had combined all the maintenance requirements into a small number of service bundles at clearly defined intervals. The service bundles were posted on a large display, showing the mileage at which each bundle was recommended, and the base price for each package. It was about as complicated as ordering an Extra Value Meal at McDonald's.

The team discovered that the Honda dealers did not relegate service to second-rate status. Rather, they used it as a marketing tool. They mailed notifications to their customers, reminding them that their next service was due and encouraging them to have it done at a Honda dealership. The language suggested that a Honda automobile is a precision piece of machinery that should be maintained regularly and only by the Honda service experts who knew the cars best. One of the growth team members, whose wife drove a Honda, brought in a mailer she had received from her dealer. The headline warned, "Don't let strangers under your hood."

The team quickly saw that, at Honda, service was far more than an ancillary profit center, it was a crucial part of the sales and marketing cycle. The customers buy the cars. The salesperson explains the standard service bundles, shows the customers the service department, and introduces them to a service adviser. The service adviser reviews the scheduled maintenance and gathers the customers' contact information. The service reminders are mailed at the appropriate intervals. When the car reaches a certain mileage the service rep alerts the sales department, and they start communicating with the customers about new models and financing options.

Now the Ford growth team began to see the service operation as an opportunity, rather than as a problem to be fixed. Their research showed that the Ford dealership system had more than sixty thousand service bays and that they were operating at 60 percent capacity, primarily with warranty work, which was profitable for the dealer, but not for Ford. If a hotel operated with a 60 percent occupancy rate it would soon be out of business. The growth team determined that if Ford could beat Honda's retention rate—or even come close—its dealers' service bays would be humming along at full capacity.

Furthermore, improving its dealership service operations would be an indirect attack on Midas, Pep Boys, and Jiffy Lube. If Ford could build a better service relationship with its customers, it could steal business from the Main Street retailers, almost unnoticed.

Although the opportunity looked good, some members of the growth team were reluctant to become imitators. At a crucial meeting, just before a decision on whether to adopt the Honda model, one of the team members looked pained. "So, after all this work, and all this analysis, we're just going to copy Honda?" he asked. There was an awkward silence. Then one of the team members broke the silence, and said, "Don't shade your eyes. Plagiarize." It was a reference to a song by Tom Lehrer, a mathematician and satirist, about the best way to get ahead in mathematics.

The Ford team voted to move forward with the bundled service plan.

REPLICATING THE HONDA HEARTBEAT

Now came time for execution, which is especially difficult when it involves asking a proud organization to copy the practices of a well-known rival. It is difficult, if not impossible, to get people who believe in their work and respect their organizations to simply copy anyone's ideas or mimic the practices of another company. They will join the effort, however, if they believe they can improve on the original idea and make it their own.

It would be easy to reproduce the tangible aspects of the Honda offering—the service bundles and the service reminder mailings—but the challenge would come in getting Ford's dealers to follow in Honda's ideological footsteps. Honda dealers truly believed in the importance of service to their business. The Ford organization saw service as a secondary business or even as an annoyance. Ford dealers had allowed the "Fix It Right First Time" plan to atrophy and the Ford Auto Care idea hadn't gained much traction. But this plan was different. The growth team had done their homework, understood the magnitude of the opportunity, and wanted to win. In order to do that, they had to get all their people to realize that service was a game worth playing.

The first hurdle in perception-changing was a high one: Ford's engineers. They were career car guys and purists when it came to engineering issues. They believed that every part had a specific life expectancy. If one part was designed to be replaced at sixty thousand miles and another at sixty-five thousand miles that's what the customer should be advised to do. "I don't care if they actually do it," said one engineer. "But it's our job to tell them what's best for the car." Decades of that kind of thinking had resulted in a total of about eighteen thousand different servicing requirements, intervals, and options.

There were heated meetings between the growth team and the engineers. Tempers rose; shouting ensued. "Put a Mustang and an F250 Super Duty Truck on the same maintenance schedule?" one engineer barked. "That's the most ridiculous thing I've ever heard." The growth team tried to explain that having eighteen thousand service intervals was just as ridiculous, and was probably contributing to the poor service loyalty rate at Ford dealerships. "Wouldn't it be better to create service bundles that customers could understand and would actually buy, rather than not doing any maintenance at all?" asked a growth team member.

The engineers held firm until the growth team found an ally, a senior executive at Ford's truck division. They invited him to attend a meeting with the engineers. The growth team explained once again that, in order to grow, the service process had to start with the needs of the customer, not with the obsessions of the engineers. They described Honda's simplified service packages. Finally, in a deft piece of corporate theater, they pulled out Ford's massive service manual—packed with the eighteen thousand maintenance advisories, recommendations, guidelines, cautions, and requirements—and dropped it on the desk with a thud. The truck executive was convinced. "You're right," he said. With the support of this respected engineer and executive, the growth team began to change the perception of service within Ford.

CONVINCING THE DEALERS TO PLAY

Although the players in the corporate organization were on board with the plan, the Ford growth team still had to face their toughest and most important audience: the Ford dealers. They are a fiercely independent group, most of them highly successful, who love to sell cars but are less than thrilled about selling service. Soon after gaining approval, the growth team decided to make a live presentation to the most influential Ford dealers at a Dealers Council meeting in Atlanta. "We had one shot at them," said a member of the growth team. "We knew we had to present a convincing program and show the dealers what was in it for them."

Well before the meeting, members of the growth team visited each of the key dealerships to gather sales data and other information. Back at the office, they created a forecasting model for each dealership, and used it to calculate how much an increase in customer loyalty would contribute to the dealer's bottom line.

At the meeting, the team talked the dealers through just three slides—the customer loyalty comparisons, the elements of the Honda service approach, and the customer sales and ownership life cycle. They told the dealers that Ford could create decisive advantage if they brought service into their strategy. Ford sells the car to the customer. Ford gets to know the customer and his needs. Ford has the first shot at gaining his service loyalty. Other maintenance providers and garages don't have this advantage. They meet the customer only when he needs a routine maintenance or has a service problem. In short, service is Ford's business to lose.

The lights came up. A Ford executive sat down next to each dealer and, together, they looked at the forecasting model on a laptop and reviewed the dealer's service results. The numbers spoke even more eloquently than the presenters had. The dealers realized they could take in as much as $200,000 more in annual service revenue, with almost no additional expense.

The growth team nudged the dealers toward a decision. "We didn't want to embarrass them," one growth team member explained. "Dealers are proud. We had to get them to say, 'I'm crazy not to do this.'" By the end of the meeting, the Dealers Council had endorsed bundled service.

With the approval of their most influential dealers, the Ford team presented the initiative to the entire dealer system. "We knew we had to do it fast," recalled a team member. "We had to complete the launch in less than a year or our management would pull the plug on the effort. We also had to be fundamental. This thing really had to work or we were going to be dead meat."

The team grabbed Ford managers from other programs to help, scraped up money from wherever they could, and pushed themselves to the limits of their energy. They took a road show to two hundred locations nationwide and met with some four thousand dealers. They were more successful than they had hoped; more than 3,400 of them signed on. They posted the service package boards, sent out service reminders to their customers, and most important, integrated the program into their sales efforts.

For four straight years, Ford's Customer Service Division achieved double-digit growth. Just as Ford had expected, the indirect attack stole business from Midas, Pep Boys, and the independent garages. The strategy worked so well that FCSD expanded the maintenance offering to include tire replacement. In its first twelve months, FCSD's tire business grew from next to nothing to a million tires.

Through their earlier, and unsuccessful, efforts at adaptation, Ford had learned that it's never enough to copy the details of someone else's successful program. It's essential that your organization create it anew and develop genuine passion for it. The growth team felt the passion when they did their research and realized the size of the opportunity. The engineers felt it when they realized that bundled service was better for their beloved cars than no maintenance at all. And dealers felt the passion when they saw they were leaving a lot of money on the table that could be theirs with a simple shift of approach.

PRACTICES AND PITFALLS OF TAKING IDEAS

Adapting an idea from a competitor may sound easy. It isn't. A good idea for your competitor, or a company in a different industry, may not fit your own business model at all. It may not bring you competitive advantage. It may even cause you to fail and go out of business.

Copy only when it will enable you to gain leadership. Whether taking ideas from within your industry or from outside it, copying requires the identification of a practice that, if truly understood and successfully transplanted, has the potential to dramatically improve the performance of your business.

If you find a way to adopt a practice, you must use the borrowed idea to become a leader, particularly vis-à-vis the competitor from whom you took the idea. If you don't, you will find yourselves in a stalemate. Or, worse, you will be seen as an inept copier, a me-too company that couldn't even pilfer properly. Think of all the second-rate fast food chains that borrowed the McDonald's idea but can't beat them with it— from national chains like Hardee's to the countless regional chains and mom and pops. IBM and Kodak mindlessly plagiarized copiers and ended up with me-too products. Kmart copied The Home Depot in creating Builders' Square, which not only brought them no competitive advantage, it caused them major headaches. Minor cost reductions or incremental quality improvements are nice, but they're not worth copying if all they'll get for you is second or third place and a reputation as a knock-off.

Borrow when it will facilitate the indirect attack. Hardballers try to avoid direct competition, and they adapt from others only when it will enable an indirect strategy. Ricoh changed the game in copiers with an indirect attack on Xerox. Ricoh copied Xerox's machines, but sold them through small distributors to small businesses, gaining a competitive advantage with price and limited service. Xerox scarcely reacted to the attack, believing that its big machines and service orientation would continue to give them competitive advantage. But when the Xerox leases ended, Xerox lost customers and its copier business suffered.

Copy completely, commit fully. The most common way to go astray is to copy the model incompletely and not commit fully to it. Halfway copying may create tortuous conflicts and inconsistencies for your organization, processes, and people.

The airlines are particularly prone to this form of inept plagiarism and their favorite paragon is Southwest Airlines. Continental Airlines copied first, launching CALight in 1993, and changing its name to Continental Lite in 1994. Like Southwest, Continental Lite offered frequent departures, low fares, fast boarding and deplaning, and no-frills service. They had initial success and, at its peak, Lite represented one-third of Continental's seat capacity. But then Lite cratered. Continental fired the CEO, took a write-off, and shut down operations in 1995.

What went wrong? Although Continental Lite copied certain aspects of the Southwest model, it retained many others of its parent. For example, Lite continued Continental's practice of paying commissions to travel agents, but cut the percentage, angering the agents and jeopardizing service. Lite used the Continental frequent flyer program, but offered fewer benefits, which confused and annoyed customers of both airlines. Lite offered assigned seats, a practice that slowed down boarding and deplaning. It allowed luggage transfers, which made for longer gate stays, increased the opportunity to lose luggage and disappoint passengers, and created a reliance on the airport system, further slowing things down. And, like its parent, it flew a mixed fleet of aircraft, which increased the costs of training, maintenance, and scheduling. Lite had drawn the Southwest face on its airline, but had failed to transplant the heart of its business model.

Make the copy your own. It is possible to completely copy a successful model and still introduce differences and characteristics that give the new version its own distinct identity.

Ryanair is the one airline that has imitated Southwest without looking like a pale shadow of the original. Founded in 1985, Ryanair struggled along for several years flying passengers from Waterford, Ireland, to London-Gatwick. The airline grew modestly until a new management team, with the exuberant Michael O'Leary as deputy CEO, took over in 1990. In that year, O'Leary journeyed to Texas to meet with Herb Kelleher, founder of Southwest, and returned to Ireland determined to follow the Southwest model. That meant transforming the small, traditional airline into a no-frills provider, with a single class of service, operating with no unions and no travel agents, flying routes to second-tier inexpensive airports, and with a fleet composed exclusively of the world's most popular airplane, the 737. Oh yes, and the fares would be dramatically low—as little as $27 one way from London to Rome.

Ryanair has become a smashing success. In their fiscal year 2002–2003, the airline achieved a 59 percent increase in after-tax profits, on a 35 percent increase in revenue. In 2001 and 2002, they more than doubled the number of passenger manifests. One competitor said that Ryanair should not be called a "low-cost airline" but rather a "high-margin airline."[4]

What has Ryanair done right? Most important, they copied the Southwest model completely and committed to it with zeal. Of course, as a small regional airline, they did not have the legacy or complexity that Continental had, which made the transformation easier. Michael O'Leary also has the ability to energize his people and imbue his airline with the same kind of electricity and sense of mission that Herb Kelleher has put into Southwest. O'Leary listened to the heartbeat of Southwest and replicated it at Ryanair.

Hardball players are not afraid to pick up on what others have done. And it's a good thing. Steve Jobs knew he was looking at a good thing when he saw an early version of a Graphical User Interface at Xerox Palo Alto Research Center (PARC). If he had ignored it, would Apple exist?

What if Kiichiro Toyoda had not applied the just-in-time techniques he learned from Ford?

Hardball competitors seize on a good idea when they see one and then they add something to the model—improve it, adapt it, or interpret it. Soon enough, what might have been seen as copying looks like innovation.

SIX

Entice Your Competitor into Retreat

In certain circumstances, it is possible to entice your competitor into retreat from competing in a business area that is important and highly profitable for you. This can be done by taking actions that are likely to lure your competitor into a different business area where you also may both compete, but that is less important and profitable for you. One of the best ways to entice a competitor to retreat from your main area of interest into another area is to leverage your superior knowledge of the costs of your business activities. If you can lure your competitor to compete in an area that it believes (because of its inferior knowledge of its costs) is highly profitable for it, but, in fact, is not, you may be able to nudge it out of the area of your greatest profitability, and also cause its costs to go up, its margins to shrink, and its share to decline. You have, in effect, led your competitor to a business area that it convinces itself is the entrance to a goldmine but, is, in fact, a rabbit hole. This form of indirect attack is the most complex and subtle of all the hardball strategies, and requires a superior understanding of both your own and your competitors' costs and pricing.

Japanese manufacturers masterfully used a version of this strategy to attack and gain power in many industries in Western markets in the 1970s and 1980s. The Japanese company would build a base in the high-volume segment of the market, typically the low end. Their

Western competitors, thinking that the low end of the market was not profitable enough to fight for, would respond by adding features to their offerings that would justify a price increase rather than by trying to cut their own prices or lower their costs. Eventually, they would abandon the segment altogether and focus their efforts on the higher-end products, which generally resulted in their losing overall market share.

Once the Western competitors had retreated from the low end, the Japanese companies would attack again, usually in the higher-priced segment where their competitors had taken refuge. As they gradually moved up the range, they would control their costs in such a way that they could always keep their prices lower than those of their Western competitors' offerings.

As the Japanese companies became more and more expert at conquering the market, segment by higher segment, the Western competitors became more and more skilled at deluding themselves that they were outfoxing the Japanese by relinquishing to them the less valuable, commodity portion of the market, while capturing the lucrative, higher-margin business for themselves. They believed that the Japanese companies did not have the technology or capability to challenge them in these segments.

These Western competitors were ignorant of the effects of experience on cost and generally had inadequate knowledge of their own costs. They didn't understand that, as the Japanese companies' unit volume grew, their cost per unit steadily declined, as they used their accumulated experience to take costs out of their products. And, as the Western competitors added features and complexity to their products, and unit volume shrank, their cost per unit steadily increased. The Japanese companies also benefited from their mastery of quality, which enabled them to steadily reduce their manufacturing costs, regardless of volume. It also resulted in improved product quality, so they could achieve low "in-service" costs—those costs associated with warranty fulfillment, service, and repair.

Gradually, the quality of Japanese products raised the expectations of consumers. Although many of the Western companies began efforts to improve, they could not match Japanese quality overnight, and so had to commit more resources to in-service performance—boosting service, allowing more warranty repairs, and accepting no-questions-asked returns. These activities further increased their costs to the point that many Western manufacturers could not raise their prices enough to cover costs. They exited the business or retreated to specialty niches.

Some of the industries where Japanese companies gained decisive advantage by raising their competitors' costs include:

- *Ball bearings.* Koyo Seiko, Nippon Seiko (NSK), and Toyo Bearings led the Japanese assault on Western manufacturers, including Sweden's SKF and Germany's FAG, by focusing on a narrow product offering in the high-volume automotive market.

- *Motorcycles.* Honda, and later Yamaha and Suzuki, gutted the markets of Western manufacturers such as Norton, Triumph, and Harley-Davidson by starting with small, low-priced motorcycles and then progressively moving upscale as the Western manufacturers retreated to bigger and higher-priced products.

- *Machine tools.* Yamazaki and other Japanese manufacturers chased Cincinnati Milacron, Ingersoll Rand, and others into the upscale portion of the market by introducing simple, low-priced, high-quality machine tools.

- *Copiers.* Ricoh and Canon entered the office copier market with low-priced machines that had limited features—products that Western competitors such as Xerox did not offer. Demand took off, allowing the Japanese to invest in creating products with more features and move into the heart of Xerox's line.

The strategy that these Japanese companies employed so successfully in the 1980s can be applied in almost any industry and market, just as Federal-Mogul, an auto parts manufacturer, did to overcome a rival, JP Industries (JPI), in the early 1990s.

FEDERAL-MOGUL SEEKS TO STEM A DECLINE IN PROFITABILITY

Federal-Mogul, with current annual sales of about $5 billion, had been suffering a decline in profitability and went looking for ways to improve it.[1]

At the time, Federal-Mogul sold to three main groups of customers in North America. The first group was the big original equipment manufacturers (OEMs), including Ford and General Motors, which bought large quantities of many different kinds of parts for production of their new vehicles. The second group was composed of a number of smaller OEMs—including John Deere, Cummins Engine Company, Caterpillar, and Navistar, as well as the heavy-duty vehicle divisions of GM and Ford—which bought fewer different parts and in smaller quantities. The third group consisted of repair shops, independent distributors, and other aftermarket players, all of which bought small quantities of parts.

Each group of customers had a different buying style and different relationships with and value to Federal-Mogul. The big OEMs put tremendous pressure on all their suppliers to keep prices low, and then lower them some more. But Federal-Mogul, and other suppliers like it, competed fiercely for this thin-margin business because they knew that high-volume production enabled them to lower their costs. Even more important, sales to the big OEMs gave them entry to the aftermarket, where they could sell a wide range of parts at much higher margins. Components suppliers offered prices to the OEMs that were scarcely above cost so they could wag the long "tail" of higher-margin, aftermarket business. Federal-Mogul did not wish to exit this business, but it did not see a way to increase its profitability.

It did see an opportunity, however, with the second group of customers, the smaller OEMs. These customers, although buying in lower volumes than the big OEMs, typically paid a higher price per unit, which made for a better gross margin. These OEMs also gave Federal-Mogul an in to the lucrative aftermarket. It decided to put its energies into increasing sales to these low-volume customers, particularly of engine bearings.

Federal-Mogul pursued its strategy for about eighteen months, and was successful in winning more business in low-volume orders for engine bearings. However, the increased sales did not improve its profitability, as it had hoped they would. Frustrated and perplexed, Dennis Gormley, Federal-Mogul's CEO, set out to discover what was going on. If the company was selling more parts to these customers, each with a higher profit per unit, why weren't its overall profits going up?

Gormley and his team found the answer to their question in an unexpected place. The manufacturing cost-accounting system, although a state-of-the-art, industry-standard system, was giving Federal-Mogul an inaccurate picture of total costs relative to volume. The system accurately tracked the direct costs—material, machine time, and direct labor—of manufacturing each part. But it had been designed to total all the indirect costs of production—including depreciation, indirect labor (machine set-up, maintenance, material handling, and supervision), and inventory—and then allocate an average cost to every part. As a result, the low-volume parts appeared to be cheaper to produce than they actually were. Federal-Mogul had been basing its prices on this inaccurate cost calculation. When it understood the true cost, Federal-Mogul realized, to its horror, that it had, in some cases, been selling its engine bearings at below cost. No wonder its profitability had not increased.

It might as well have been shipping cash to its smaller OEM customers.

A RIVAL PROVIDES AN INSPIRATION

Federal-Mogul considered the possibility of raising prices on their existing low-volume engine bearing contracts. But they were afraid the customers would dump them and take their business to a particularly nettlesome rival, JP Industries (JPI).

JPI, a U.S. company, was part of T&N PLC, a British conglomerate that was the biggest supplier of automotive parts in Europe. Although the parent company had plenty of high-volume business in Europe, in the competition for the big OEMs' business in the United States, its JPI unit was more of an annoyance than a serious threat. Federal-Mogul, armed with the superior cost position provided by its greater scale in the high-volume business, won the vast majority of these contracts.

JPI competed aggressively, however, for the low-volume engine bearing business to smaller OEMs. What's more, their pricing was inconsistent, and they often undercut Federal-Mogul's bids. This was puzzling, because JPI was not significantly larger than Federal-Mogul in the low-volume business and therefore should not have had a cost advantage.

Federal-Mogul's managers concluded that JPI must be desperate for cash flow. This was plausible, because JPI had grown through a series of acquisitions and had racked up huge debts in the process. Yet their production costs were probably low, because JPI was running older equipment that had been fully depreciated.

The Federal-Mogul management team debated the pros and cons of raising prices on low-volume engine bearing orders to the smaller OEMs. Many believed that the business, even if it was only marginally profitable, was important because it helped cover overhead. They also believed that if Federal-Mogul gave away any business to JPI it would quickly lose share and eventually JPI would take over the low-volume business completely. Finally, Dennis Gormley decided that Federal-Mogul could not continue to lose money on its low-volume business. It had to seek a price increase on existing low-volume engine bearing contracts.

Seeking a price increase, especially on existing contracts, is almost unheard of in the automotive business. Generally, it works the other way around—the OEMs come to their suppliers looking for a price decrease before the contract has run its course. But Gormley knew that Federal-Mogul had some clout. It was the leading player in the industry and had longstanding relationships with most of its customers. Most important, Gormley knew that the costs of switching from Federal-Mogul to another supplier would be high. The customer would have to go through the complex process of identifying and qualifying a new supplier, which often required providing capital for new tools, undergoing a lengthy process of testing the products against specifications, and building inventory. Even with these advantages, Gormley decided that the best way to minimize the number of customer defections would be for him to personally lobby the key accounts.

At General Motors, where Federal-Mogul supplied engine bearings to the low-volume diesel-engine businesses, Gormley made his case to Rick Wagoner, who was then head of North America. "I had a meeting with Rick and ten of his closest friends from purchasing," Gormley recalled. "When I told him how much we were losing on some of GM's business, he asked, 'Is it really that bad?' I told him that his business was costing us five cents a share in earnings. He said, 'Okay.' And that was that."

To Gormley's surprise, most of the other OEMs also went along with the price hike on their existing contracts. "The customers accepted our analysis," Gormley said. "They didn't like the price increase. But the thought of qualifying a supplier to replace Federal-Mogul was even less attractive."

Once they had resolved the problem of the money-losing contracts on low-volume business, Gormley turned once again to the original question: how to increase profitability.

Now that they knew the actual cost of producing low-volume orders, they could set prices accordingly on future contracts. They might lose more of the bids, but the loss might be more than offset by the higher profit per part. They did not yet know, however, how a decrease in the number of orders of the low-volume products would affect the profitability of their high-volume business. Perhaps profitability of those orders would decline and wipe out any increase in profits from the low-volume business.

The positive aspect of the cost-accounting revelations was that Federal-Mogul now knew that the high-volume parts were actually cheaper for it to produce than it had thought. As a result, it felt that they had an unexpected profit cushion. If the high-volume OEMs came looking for price concessions during the life of the contract, the company could absorb them better than it might have thought.

Gormley and his team wondered if there was a way to use their new knowledge of cost and pricing to accomplish their objective of increasing profitability. Most suppliers used the same manufacturing cost accounting system that had been leading Federal-Mogul astray. It was likely, therefore, that JPI did not understand the true cost of manufacturing low-volume parts. After all, their fixed costs were very low because of the amortized equipment. If the accounting system was allocating a low indirect cost to each part, JPI probably thought that its costs were much lower than they really were. It probably believed, as Federal-Mogul had formerly believed, that its low-volume business was far more profitable than it really was.

Then the Federal-Mogul team had a clever, almost wickedly clever, idea. Suppose Federal-Mogul were to intentionally overprice its bids on low-volume engine bearing business. JPI would probably win more of the low-volume contracts when bidding against Federal-Mogul. Soon enough, JPI would realize that Federal-Mogul was losing because they had raised their prices. JPI might be emboldened to raise its prices, at least a little, but not enough to be truly profitable. Thanks to its greater number of wins against Federal-Mogul, JPI's low-volume business would grow. Its management would assume—thanks to its inaccurate cost-accounting system—that the low-volume business was contributing much more profit than it actually was. It would probably then be enticed into pursuing even more low-volume orders. Its costs would rise. Its profitability would fall. But it wouldn't know why. Or, at least, not right away.

Even more delicious to contemplate was that, as JPI's costs rose and its profitability fell, its cost-accounting system would likely identify JPI's high-volume business as the culprit, because it would show the gross margin of the high-volume business to be lower than that of its low-volume business. As a result, JPI might raise prices on its high-volume bids and Federal Mogul could easily undercut JPI, if it wanted or needed to, thus further building its high-volume business.

GAINING ADVANTAGE BY RESTRAINING THE KILLER IMPULSE

Federal-Mogul now had a competitive advantage over JPI. Thanks to its superior understanding of its costs, it could price its bids high enough on low-volume business that, if it won the contract, it would be slightly profitable. If it lost the contract to a supplier, like JPI, that offered a lower price, it would probably not be profitable for that competitor. The keener understanding of costs also enabled Federal-Mogul to be more aggressive in its pricing of high-volume products, which would lead to winning more contracts, which would build its volume, and further reduce its costs.

There was, however, a danger lurking in this strategy: Federal-Mogul's own competitive instinct. It was very likely that Federal-Mogul could build its competitive advantage into decisive advantage and, conceivably, lure JPI so far down the rabbit hole that it could not escape. JPI was, after all, financially unstable. It might not realize what was happening to it—and take steps to change its strategy—before it came to the brink of disaster. Dennis Gormley knew that his team, conditioned by their long history of competing in a cutthroat industry with high fixed costs, had come to believe that there was nothing better than winning business, no matter how thin the margin. Gormley realized that now things had to be different; sometimes it would be better to lose a bid against JPI.

Gormley did not want JPI to be so weakened by their rising costs that it could declare bankruptcy, or that it might give up, exit the market, or sell the business. With bankruptcy protection, or under a new owner who could write down the value of JPI's assets, dealing with JPI might get even crazier for Federal-Mogul. JPI could probably lower costs even further and, when faced with extinction, might attack Federal-Mogul's high-volume business. "We wanted to keep them on the ropes, earning just enough money to stay in business," Gormley said. "We used pricing as a way to attract them to business we didn't want and to stay away from the business we did want."

So Federal-Mogul continued to bid for low-volume business, setting its prices just high enough that it lost most competitions but low enough to keep JPI's profit margins slim. To keep JPI from catching on to the scheme, Federal-Mogul would occasionally price its bids so it could win a low-volume order. Now and again, it would also let JPI win an order in the high-volume business. However, Federal-Mogul used its pricing tactics to keep JPI away from the most important orders on its biggest moneymaking products in the high-volume segment.

FEDERAL-MOGUL DISCOVERS THAT EVEN LEADERSHIP HAS LIMITS

Federal-Mogul's quest for increased profitability was just one aspect of a larger strategy: It wished to become the leading global player in its industry, not just the North American leader. Although their business with the U.S. automakers was strong, Federal-Mogul had no contracts with the Japanese manufacturers, nor did it have much of a presence in Europe. Gormley decided that the only way for Federal-Mogul to grow was for it to become the worldwide supplier of choice, with the lowest costs and highest quality. The pricing strategy on low-volume business worked as planned and contributed to Federal-Mogul's larger success. By 2000, Federal-Mogul was the major supplier of engine bearings to BMW, Mercedes, GM, and Ford, and was winning some contracts with the Japanese automakers. It had also reversed the decline in profitability.

But then things turned sour. Federal-Mogul instituted a cost-reduction program that did not produce results as quickly as the directors had hoped. The recession cut into its business. It made a push into auto-parts retailing that ran into problems. Although profitability had improved, it wasn't improving fast enough to satisfy the directors. In 1996, they asked for Gormley's resignation.

Richard Snell, Gormley's successor, decided to seek growth and increased profitability through acquisitions. Federal-Mogul decided to purchase T&N PLC, JPI's parent, which manufactured a range of auto components, including brake pads. Federal-Mogul had previously considered the purchase of T&N, encouraged by investment bankers who believed there would be "perfect synergy" between the two companies. But Gormley had decided against the purchase because T&N was involved in a number of legal actions involving asbestos, a material used in brake pads. Gormley believed that T&N's liabilities could grow very large, much larger than the investment bankers' estimates. But Richard Snell decided to take the risk. He lost. T&N's liabilities grew so onerous that Federal-Mogul was forced to seek bankruptcy protection.

Even so, the engine bearings business that Gormley had so carefully built and protected through hardball pricing, continues to thrive.

RECOGNIZING AN OPPORTUNITY TO RAISE YOUR COMPETITOR'S COSTS

The kind of hardball attack that Federal-Mogul employed against JPI can be launched by companies in almost any industry, but for it to be a success, the company must be properly prepared and the conditions must be right.

Opportunities arise most often in industries where there is enough complexity that the competitor may not know the true cost of producing one or more of their products. We have seen such opportunities in many different kinds of industries, including life insurance, private branch exchanges (PBX's), distribution, commercial aircraft, and real estate development. As different as these industries are, they have similar characteristics:

- *The main competitors have a broad range of product or service offerings.* They have complex, multistep manufacturing processes and service-delivery systems.

- *There are very large differences in the sales volumes of the various products offered by the main competitors.* Some products sell in extremely large volumes, others in very small numbers of units. There are also very large differences in the sales volumes by customer. A few customers place massive orders. Many others place much smaller orders. Because of these disparities in volumes there are large cost differences, making it much harder for the company to allocate costs accurately to a specific product or order.

- *There are significant indirect costs.* As we saw in the Federal-Mogul example, it is very difficult to allocate indirect costs—including SG&A (Selling, General, and Administrative), factory overhead, and customer service—to specific products, especially when you produce many different products, and in widely varying quantities. When indirect costs exceed 50 percent of value-added costs, the possibility of misallocation is very high. (Value added costs are the cost of all the internal activities that a company undertakes to transform incoming materials into finished products.)

- *The indirect costs that are most difficult to allocate accurately are those associated with creating and managing customer relationships.* These include the costs of making sales, providing maintenance and service, handling special orders, taking returns, and offering individualized financing or payment terms. When these indirect costs are high, the sales to some customers will appear to be more profitable than they actually are.

- *The compensation of certain employees, usually those in sales and marketing, is tied to the contributions their efforts make to the gross margin.* Such compensation incentives can make these employees pay more attention to customers who will pay the highest prices. Although the gross margins of such customers tend to be high, the service costs may also be very high and are often misallocated.

- *Competition is based primarily on price.* Such environments are ripe for using price to exploit a competitor's flawed understanding of the true costs of serving different segments.

- *The industry is in a rapid growth phase.* When an industry is booming, management practices get sloppy. With sales and profits rising fast, many companies won't focus on careful cost accounting and have only a general idea of the cost of producing specific products. They may not notice, or may choose to ignore, the pricing moves made by a hardball competitor.

- *There are not too many competitors, but not too few, either.* In an industry with only two or three main competitors, each company is usually very aware of the others' actions, making it difficult to make an unnoticed indirect attack. In an industry with many competitors (five or more), it is very difficult for one competitor to taking pricing actions that will influence the behavior of all the others in the desired ways. If a company attacks one rival, the other competitors may take actions that deflect it. For example, if Federal-Mogul had had several rivals and they chose to compete aggressively for the low-volume business, JPI might not have won enough orders to weaken them.

PREPARATIONS FOR A PRICING ATTACK AND POTHOLES TO AVOID

The first step in preparing to raise your competitor's costs is to deaverage your own. Activities and operations that serve low-volume customers should be disaggregated from those that serve high-volume customers, so that each facility, process, and service is dedicated to one type or the other. For most companies, this allows management to get an accurate picture of the true costs and profits generated by each customer category, account, product, and service.

Cost disaggregation can be difficult to accomplish. Some customers may purchase both high-volume and low-volume products, and it may be beneficial for the company to present a single face to those customers and to have a comprehensive view of the account. If disaggregation is onerously difficult or will jeopardize customer relationships, it may be that raising a competitor's costs is not an appropriate strategy for you.

If your own costs can be disaggregated, the next step is to analyze your competitor's cost structure and pricing behavior. This is best done by identifying the differences between you and your competitor, such as facilities and equipment, complexity, and volumes, and estimate the difference between your costs and your competitor's costs.

Next, because you have already determined how your own costs have been misallocated, you can make an informed judgment about where your competitor may be misallocating his. Then you can determine how these misallocations are likely to be distorting your competitor's perceptions of the profitability of specific products or customers. By looking at the prices your competitor is actually charging for those products, you'll have a good indication of where his pricing does not correlate properly with his true costs.

Once you know if your competitor is vulnerable to a pricing attack, you need to determine exactly what you want the attack to achieve. Do you want to influence your competitor so that he raises prices with a certain type of customer? Do you want to keep the competitor away from all customers who buy a certain product? Keep the needs and well-being of your customers firmly in mind as you set your objective. Hardball players wish to weaken their competitors, but they never want to weaken or harm their customers.

Once you have determined your objective, you must choose a cost-raising strategy to achieve it. Such strategies include:

- *Strengthen your grip on customers that purchase in high volumes at prices that result in low margins.* These are often the most important customers to win and keep because their high volumes can be key to achieving low costs. Prices for these customers must be set so that you can win as much of their business as possible. At the same time, you need to reduce the cost of serving these customers, to increase your margin.

- *Shed customers that purchase low volumes at low prices.* These are undesirable customers, but they may seem desirable to competitors who have a poor understanding of their costs and those that have a culture that values winning above all. You want to set your prices high enough that your competitors will win most of this business, but not so high that they will make substantial profit.

- *Retain low-volume customers that pay high prices, but be ready to ditch them if their willingness to pay erodes.* Such customers will be profitable until the competition notices them and undercuts your price. Pretty soon these customers will become undesirable low-volume, low-price customers. Then you should set prices that will encourage your competitors to bid for and win their business.

- *Retain high-volume customers that pay high net prices.* Such customers are rare and you should cultivate and enjoy their business as long as you can. Once competition comes—and it will—strive to retain these customers and keep your prices as high as possible by raising their costs of switching. This can be done by increasing service, assuming some of the customer's value-added steps, or offering price incentives that encourage volume purchase and a long-term relationship.

- *Offer incentives to your important customers who purchase both high- and low-volume products.* A customer who buys primarily high-volume, low-margin goods from you may also have a need for low-volume, high-margin products and services. You might offer these customers an incentive, such as a discount, to buy both high-volume and low-volume products from you, but make it clear to the customer that the discount is available on the low-volume business only as long as he continues to send you his high-volume orders.

Whichever strategy you follow, you must also work to reduce your costs by redesigning products and processes. The combination of your increased volume, higher profits, and lower costs—along with your competitor's rising costs—can create a powerful competitive advantage. If you can achieve the lowest manufacturing and service costs, and create greater cash flows than those of your competitors—so that you have more money to reinvest in your business—you may be able to attain decisive advantage.

There are significant risks involved when trying to raise a competitor's costs. Your insights into costs, pricing, and behavior have to be accurate. Execution must be bold. Small mistakes can jeopardize the whole effort.

An attempt to become the leading force in the high-volume segment and raise competitors' costs by moving them toward high-margin, low-volume customers is a bet-the-company strategy. You will be intentionally giving up certain kinds of business in order to build other kinds. If you don't win the customers you have targeted, you may see a plunge in both the top and bottom lines.

Once you have embarked on a cost-raising strategy, you have to be careful that it doesn't become irrelevant. It is possible to win so much high-volume business and get your costs so low that you can reduce prices beyond the point where the customer cares. When the price gets low enough, customers begin to care more about other factors, such as features and performance. Customers will then pay a premium for those more attractive products, and the low-volume business will become more profitable than the high-volume business.

Texas Instruments (TI) fell into the irrelevance trap in calculators and watches. By relentlessly building volume, driving down costs, and lowering prices, TI achieved leading market share in both products. Retail prices for watches and calculators plunged below $15, and TI dominated the volume channels, including supermarkets and discount stores.

Casio, Sharp, and Seiko—all Japanese companies—followed TI's lead in pursuing volume by slashing prices and designing costs out of the products and their manufacturing. But, as prices sank, the Japanese companies introduced new products with many more features than TI's offerings. Prices were so low, consumers were willing to pay a few dollars extra for features such as solar power, more mathematical functions for calculators, and styling features for watches. Before long, TI's relentless pursuit of higher volumes and lower costs became irrelevant to consumers, and the Japanese companies took over the categories.

If you have not examined your costs, in detail, within the past five years—or if you believe your competitors have not—it is very likely that there exists, lurking somewhere in your cost structure, a major opportunity to improve your profits, weaken your competitor, and expand your influence.

There are limits to cost-raising strategy. As important as price is to your customers, they care about other things as well, including product features, quality, time, and status. So, even as you pursue this hardball strategy with gusto, remember the mortal words of Dirty Harry: "A man's got to know his limitations."[2]

SEVEN

Break Compromises

Breaking compromises is the most powerful hardball strategy for companies seeking breakaway growth.

The Home Depot broke the compromises inherent in the DIY (do-It-yourself) home-improvement business and achieved annual growth as high as 27 percent in an industry that had become accustomed to less than 5 percent growth. By breaking compromises in air travel, Southwest Airlines has grown seven times faster than the industry over the past decade and is among the most profitable airlines. In 1984, Chrysler introduced the minivan, breaking compromises in the auto industry, and over the next ten years, the minivan segment grew eight times faster than did the industry overall. Chrysler maintains its leadership today. (But the minivan segment, which had become Chrysler's richest profit sanctuary, is now under attack. See chapter 4.)

Senior managers at The Home Depot, Southwest, and Chrysler, had the wisdom, curiosity, and the perseverance to identify, explore, and then break the compromises their industries had forced customers to endure. By doing so, they released so much trapped value that they stimulated significant sales and profit growth.

What are compromises? To understand compromises, they must be differentiated from choices. Customers are accustomed to, and want, choices. They want to be able to choose from among a variety of products or services with different features, characteristics, and prices. In textiles, for example, the customer can choose from a huge range of fabrics, differentiated by such characteristics as thread count, type of yarn (cotton, nylon, wool, cashmere, etc.), color, and pattern. When looking for a hotel, the customer can choose from among many different kinds of offerings, including luxury resorts, full-service downtown hotels, no-frills business hotels, motels, all-suites, lodges, and more. In each case, the customers understand that the price will vary depending on the features and quality of the product choice they make.

A compromise, by contrast, is a limitation on customer choice made by the industry. In fabrics, for example, the customer rarely has a choice about the width of the fabric. It is governed by the capability of the looms that are standard in the industry. In hotels, the customer is informed of the standard check-in time, usually 3 P.M., which is determined by the schedule of the housekeeping staff. When such compromises are endemic to an industry, customers don't even see them as compromises. They accept them as "the way the industry works."

Consider auto repair. When would most customers choose to take their cars in for service? On the weekend. When do most dealers and garages provide service? Monday through Friday. Only recently have some dealers begun to do vehicle repair on weekends, but only on Saturday and often just a few hours in the morning. The customer does not have a choice in the matter. That's the way the car repair industry has always worked.

Customers are surrounded by compromises. Why should a home owner have to go through a costly remortgage when his mortgageholder lowers interest rates? They shouldn't; it's a compromise created by the industry to keep customers locked in to high rates and reap fees when they switch. Some financial institutions are now offering loans that automatically adjust when interest rates drop. Why can't washers and dryers do a good job of doing laundry and also look nice as part of home decor? They can, and manufacturers are now offering washer-dryer pairs with European styling and in a range of colors.

Most compromises don't have to be. There is no law of nature that says cars can't be fixed on weekends or that hotel rooms can't be ready before 3 P.M. Compromises creep into industries in various ways. Some are imposed by standard operating practices that few industry insiders or customers question. Others stem from decisions that may make marginal economic sense for the company, if customers adjust their behaviors. The most important compromises are caused when companies lose touch with their customers. They think that because customers can't see the compromise, or don't complain about it, that they are satisfied.

Then some smart company comes along, sees the compromise, and finds a way to break it. And customers suddenly see the compromise, too, and are delighted they now have a choice.

CARMAX: BREAKING THE COMPROMISES IN USED CAR SALES

In the early 1990s, Circuit City went looking for growth and found a promising opportunity in used car retailing. It created CarMax to break the compromises customers face when they purchase a used automobile.[1]

Circuit City, the big box electronics retailer, enjoyed strong sales and earnings growth until 2000. But it has been increasingly besieged by competitors, including Best Buy (offering greater variety with less service than Circuit City) and Wal-Mart (offering less variety, less service, but lower prices). The company also had completed the rollout of its winning format throughout the United States, and organic growth slowed.

Circuit City formed a team of senior managers to identify new growth opportunities. "We looked at sporting goods, auto parts, furniture and other industries, trying to find an interesting idea," said Austin Ligon, Circuit City's senior vice president of strategic planning, and the team's leader. "Our criteria were pretty straightforward. We were looking for a large business with lots of room for growth. A business where no other strong big box player was successful, and preferably with a fragmented competitor base. A business where our retail and management skills might give us an advantage. And a market where there was a clear and significant unmet consumer need."

Ligon's team considered getting into new vehicle sales, but no automaker would sell to them, because of their existing dealer relationships. "The Big Three U.S. makers said no way," said Ligon. "The Japanese? Not in this lifetime. The large European makers said, nicht, nein, never." So the Circuit City team turned its attention to used cars.

Used car retailing met all the criteria the team had established. It is a huge category and growing fast. In North America, used car retailing is a $400 billion business. Used cars constitute the third largest consumer goods category, after food and clothing. There are now more sales of used vehicles than of new ones each year, and the demand for them is growing faster than the demand for new ones. A major reason for this change in the status of used cars is that, as new cars have improved in quality and reliability, used models are in better condition and more trouble-free. "Late-model used cars are better quality than they've ever been and they last longer than ever," said Ligon. As a result, consumers no longer think of a used car as a poor substitute for a new car; they often see it as the smart choice. Why pay full retail for a new car when you can pay 30 percent less for a one-year-old car that is as good as new, is still under warranty, and has never had a problem?

Most important, the business was riddled with customer compromises. Customers had come to think of buying a used car as difficult, distasteful, and risky—far more trying than buying a new car. They had come to believe that the industry was, by nature, sleazy. A used car salesman, by definition, had to be a fast-talking, integrity-free hustler. Used cars and people who bought them were stigmatized, and the automakers themselves had contributed to the stigma. When Chrysler introduced its K-car in the early 1980s, Roger Smith, then chairman of General Motors, was asked how GM would respond to the threat and he replied that GM's answer to the K-car was a two-year-old Oldsmobile. In 1995, a *BusinessWeek* journalist grilled the program manager for the new Ford Taurus about the car's price, which was about $2,000 higher than the previous model. "If Joe Blow can't afford to buy a new car," said the program manager, "let him buy a used one."[2]

The used car retailing business has not changed as much as the cars the retailers are selling. The customer faces many compromises. First, you have to locate a car by looking through classified ads, car buying guides, or browsing Internet sites. If you want a particular model, you will find there is a limited number available. In a large metropolitan area, for example, there might be twenty or thirty used Tauruses available. If you want a car that is less than four years old, you'll most likely find it at a new car dealer who also keeps a stock of used cars. If the car is older, it will likely be at a dealer who offers only used cars, or in the driveway of an individual seller. If you choose the dealer, you may find that the car is in poor condition or too expensive, or that it's already been sold by the time you get there. If you go with an individual, you may have to travel farther than you'd like or negotiate with a maniac.

No matter where the buyer finds the car, he will have to take a chance on quality. It will likely be out of warranty, and few dealers or owners will have maintenance records to show. Some dealers certify their vehicles, but it often doesn't mean much. In Ontario, Canada, dealers must be certified, but they determine their own criteria for certification of the cars themselves. Generally, such certification insures that the car has no broken glass, the lights and brakes work, the tires have sufficient tread, and there are no leaks in the exhaust system. These are the barest of safety necessities and things that most buyers could check for themselves. They are not the things that go bump in the night, such as water pumps, head gaskets, electrical systems, suspensions, and transmissions.

So finding and buying a used car is a difficult and unpleasant process, and it's not over once the deal is made. The buyer also has to sell, trade, trash, or donate his old vehicle, and finance, insure, and register his new one. Buyers accept compromises at every step of the way. They don't have a choice about how much information they can review for the car; they take whatever is available and accept that a used car is an unknowable quantity. They expect that the used car dealer will pressure them, not tell the truth, haggle over price, make up phony deadlines, and do whatever is best for him and his dealership. The customer knows that, if anything goes wrong with his purchase, he will have little or no recourse.

Austin Ligon's team saw parallels between the state of used car retailing in the early 1990s, and appliance and electronics retailing in the 1970s. "There was a time when stereo salesmen were considered . . . well, sleazy," said Ligon. He believed many of the approaches and capabilities Circuit City had used to revolutionize that business could be applied to used car retailing. "We decided we could think about this industry like a retailer and not like a dealer. In selling used cars, unlike new ones, the retailer doesn't have to follow franchise regulations or manufacturers' rules," said Ligon. "You can display every make side by side, put a real price on it so the consumer can compare price against price, and car against car. We thought that if we could do that, we could sell more used cars than anyone could imagine."

CarMax breaks several compromises for the customer. The first outlet opened in Richmond, Virginia, in 1993, offering about 500 used vehicles of all makes. A used car dealer typically has about 30 vehicles for sale; a large new car dealer might have 130. CarMax outlets opened later were even bigger, with 1,000 to 1,500 vehicles on the lot. So, instead of driving hundreds of miles to inspect 30 Tauruses, the customer can go to a CarMax and look at 50 of them, side by side.

Circuit City harnessed its IT system capabilities to break the knowledge compromise. Every CarMax outlet has computer kiosks where customers can access information about every vehicle in stock. They can search for vehicles by model or price, from inventory available at that location or any other CarMax outlet in the region. They can check the vehicle's specifications, features, accessories, warranties, and find its location on the lot. CarMax inspects every car, putting it through 110 performance and safety checks. There is only one vehicle in the showroom, covered with arrows showing the checkpoints and with text that explains each check. The sales reps wear CarMax uniforms and their first job is to show the kiosk to their customers and explain how to use it. "Most people want to get as much information as they can before getting involved with a sales rep," said Ligon. "We try to take away the tension and anxiety."

To help change the perception of the used car salesman, CarMax prefers to hire people who are presentable rather than those with experience in vehicle sales. They put their new hires through two weeks of training; most used car salespeople at traditional dealers get a day or two of training if they get any at all. CarMax pays their salespeople a fixed dollar amount per vehicle regardless of the price rather than the straight commission a typical vehicle salesman receives, so there is no incentive to sell the customer up. To further reduce the sales pressure, CarMax sets a fixed price for each vehicle at or below the NADA Blue book value, and there is a no-haggle guarantee.

CarMax also helps reduce the risk involved in buying a used car. Customers have a five-day return guarantee. The vehicle can be returned, no questions asked, if it has been driven less than 250 miles. Every vehicle is sold with a thirty-day warranty, and there are extended warranties available for purchase. CarMax will buy any used vehicle from the customer. They offer a variety of financing choices, and can also arrange for insurance coverage. CarMax promises that their customers can locate a vehicle, buy it, insure it, and drive away in it in less than ninety minutes.

IN SEARCH OF DECISIVE ADVANTAGE

The CarMax business model gives the company a competitive advantage. Its operations are superior and costs are lower than competitors. Currently, sales per site are fourteen times higher than the average independent dealer and eight times higher than the average new car dealer selling used cars. "We sell about five thousand cars per store," said Austin Ligon, "which is about five times what the typical new car dealer sells in total volume." Wal-Mart has put most other discounters out of business in the United States with sales per site that are twice that of its competitors. CarMax has a five to fourteen times advantage! Customers respond positively to the CarMax format, and it scores consistently higher on customer satisfaction surveys than do competing formats. Customers give CarMax good marks for enhanced variety, value, fast service, and comfort.

The question remains, however, whether CarMax can expand broadly and quickly enough to attract sufficient customers to create decisive advantage. If they could achieve national coverage overnight, there is little question that the traditional dealerships as a group would be in trouble, at least in the sale of used vehicles. The CarMax volume per site advantage drastically lowers the company's selling costs compared to traditional formats. For every doubling of volume per site, the sales cost per vehicle drops about 20 percent.

CarMax needs these large sales volumes to recover its large investment—the information system alone cost about $60 million. "CarMax typically has an inventory of about twelve thousand vehicles.

That's a lot of cars to track," said Ligon. "The system was expensive, but it gave us a big competitive advantage." Not only does the system enable CarMax to keep a larger inventory than competitors, it also helps it to increase its knowledge and increase its productivity. For example, the system tracks the incidence of mechanical problems by make and model, which helps in planning and executing repair work, boosting productivity in the facilities where CarMax inspects and reconditions the used cars. "We have reduced the time it takes to recondition a car by 40 to 50 percent," Ligon said. "This means we have fewer cars sitting out back being serviced, and more cars on the sales lot out front. The information system also shows which vehicles and colors are popular in different regions of the country, which helps us manage our inventory better."

The CarMax advantage is very difficult for competitors to challenge. No single dealer can match CarMax's investment, although a dealer conglomerate might be able to, if it chose. And, because of their histories and franchise agreements, few if any traditional dealers can hope to expand to match the CarMax scale advantage. Their dealerships are often stuck in locations that were good once but have lost their appeal due to changes in their communities or surroundings, and the management doesn't have the resources or will to move. If they do seek to move, they are often limited by franchise agreements that restrict them from operating in a same-brand dealer's territory. If they want to expand on their current location, they may not have enough real estate to accommodate it.

Even if a traditional dealer could solve these issues, the culture of the traditional dealer is very, very difficult to change. The organization is geared to get the customer into a vehicle that is available on the lot, not into the vehicle they really want. Indeed, dealer employees have developed a whole language to describe their customers, and it's not flattering. There are the "lot lizards," who waste a rep's time by inspecting every available car and taking test drive after test drive. There are the "wifie boys," the "crybabies," and the "don'na knows." To such dealerships, the customer is obviously a nuisance, not a prize.

The scope of CarMax's business, coupled with its information system and management expertise, enables the company to make better purchasing decisions and create a fast-moving product mix. Used vehicle dealers buy most of their inventory at auctions hosted by dealer associations, leasing companies, and the manufacturers. The capability to make advantageous and winning bids is based on experience, up-to-date market information, scope of knowledge, and the deep pockets needed to make large purchases. The bidder who has the largest inventory of cars, the greatest geographical coverage, and the best information about which makes and models are selling and which ones are not is in a much better position to know which cars to buy, how many of them, and how much to pay. Even if the big purchaser makes a mistake now and then, it will have less of an impact on its business than it would have on a smaller purchaser. For a company with twelve thousand cars in stock, for example, twenty cars in an undesirable color is a minor problem. For a dealer with one hundred cars in stock, even five dogs could be a disaster.

So, if CarMax can achieve nationwide coverage it may be able to turn its current competitive advantage into decisive advantage.

SURVIVING CHALLENGES FROM TRADITIONAL DEALERS AND COPIERS

Because CarMax cannot go nationwide quickly, and because of the limitations of state franchise laws, traditional auto dealers can continue to play in the business and keep denying they are dying a slow death. Traditional dealers break even or lose money on the sales of new vehicles, making most of their money on used car sales (about 75 percent of profits), service (40 percent of profits) and finance and insurance (30 percent of profits). Because CarMax concentrates on only those segments, they are in a position to use another hardball strategy—they can threaten their competitor's profit sanctuaries. Furthermore, as more and more customers buy used cars, CarMax can begin to eat into the new vehicle sales of the traditional dealers. Dealers depend on the cash flow from new car sales to cover overhead and generate tag-along revenues from accessories, finance, and insurance. If enough customers choose a CarMax used car instead of new one, dealers may start operating at a loss.

The traditional dealers are almost powerless to respond to a threat from CarMax or a CarMax imitator. What choices do they have? They can whine to the manufacturers about unfair competition, but the automakers can't do much except honor and renew their franchise agreements and not make any deals with CarMax. They can try to expand to match the CarMax economics, but we've seen how difficult this can be. They can try to undercut CarMax prices, but this will hurt their profitability and is unsustainable. They can sell to a dealer conglomerate or attempt to form one. Or, they can do nothing and hope for the best.

It doesn't matter which tactic the dealers choose; they're all softball plays. A telling example of traditional dealers playing softball—refusing to face up to the reality of their situation—was their response to CarMax's effort to sell vehicles in Dallas on Saturday and Sunday. The state's blue laws allowed the sale of vehicles on only one weekend day, but not both. To break the longstanding compromise—most customers want to be able to choose which weekend day to shop for cars—CarMax decided to challenge the law, opening their Dallas showroom all day Saturday and at noon on Sunday. An industry association, the New Car Dealers Association of Metropolitan Dallas, disapproved of the move and continued to support the weekend restriction. They said that the extended sales week would increase their overhead but not their sales, and make it difficult to hire and keep good salespeople. According to a story in the *Dallas Morning News,* the Texas Motor Vehicle Commission warned CarMax that they might be guilty of a "willful violation" if the blue law was upheld in the courts. The Texas Automobile Dealers Association sought an injunction against CarMax.

The executives at CarMax did not sit back and wait for the good old boys to get their way in court. They filed suit, asking a federal court to declare the blue law unconstitutional. "Texas law does not allow us to be fully competitive," said Austin Ligon, as quoted in the Dallas paper. "We want to operate seven days a week in every store in every state we are in. We think we present a very attractive consumer offer. Here, we are blocked from presenting that offer to consumers one day a week." Today, Sunday auto sales are no longer prohibited in Texas.

A more significant challenge to CarMax came from acquisitive auto retail conglomerates such as AutoNation and United Auto. They bought out traditional dealers at a premium and folded them into the national conglomerate.

At first, Circuit City and CarMax were not fazed by the new competition. "We understand how to expand as fast or faster than anybody in retailing," said Austin Ligon, "It takes the same thing for CarMax to expand as it does for Marriott or McDonald's or Home Depot or Wal-Mart to expand. You have to have the ability to manage the details in very thin margin business. You have to control costs better than anyone else. You have to do a better job with the consumer than anybody else and do it consistently across the stores in multiple markets. You have to do it 365 days a year, even when you're growing rapidly. We gained all that expertise in building Circuit City and achieving 20 percent growth a year for more than fifteen years. We believe we'll be able to do the same or better with CarMax. Our competitors will have to struggle more with their concepts. We have a head start over everybody else in the industry."

But AutoNation, a unit of Republic Industries, mounted a tougher attack than CarMax had anticipated. Republic is headed by Wayne Huizenga, of Blockbuster fame, who has plenty of experience in the rapid roll-out of new retail formats. If anyone could go toe-to-toe with Circuit City in rolling out the big box concept in used car retailing, it was AutoNation. Huizenga could play hardball, and Ligon knew it. AutoNation also had plenty of money, the admiration of dealers who wanted to sell out at a premium, and support from Wall Street.

"Until AutoNation showed up we felt like we were part of Stonewall Jackson's Shenandoah Valley Campaign," said Ligon. "We picked the targets and attacked. It was fun. But, after AutoNation, we felt we were in the Battle of Stalingrad. Two great armies locked in a battle to the death. There could be only one outcome, one survivor. It was scary. It was do or die!"

AutoNation forced CarMax to enter markets before it was ready. It wanted to get into the big, growth markets like Dallas and Atlanta before AutoNation could sew them up. It expanded too rapidly before they had finished testing the concept. As a result, some of the stores were too big. Operations weren't efficient. Cash flow was pressured.

But AutoNation had its own problems. It tried to play hardball by copying the CarMax concept, but made the classic softball mistake of not replicating its heartbeat. It built big inventories like CarMax and copied the layout and look of the CarMax outlets. But it did not try or were unable to change the culture and break the compromises inherent in the traditional sales process. Getting an AutoNation salesman to quote against a no-haggle price was as easy as threatening to walk! In addition, AutoNation was burdened with the new car dealerships it had acquired at big premiums, and the combination of high costs, low revenues, and weak profits in the early stages of the rollout became increasingly difficult to explain to investors.

AutoNation blinked. When a new president came in, he chose to invest in the established dealerships and strong brand names rather than shovel more money into the risky concept of big box used car retailing. At the end of 1999, AutoNation announced that all its used car superstores would be closed. CarMax had prevailed.

With the defeat of AutoNation, and the onset of recession, CarMax decided to slow the pace of expansion. It needed to fine-tune the format and improve its IT systems. It had found that not all markets could support the original superstore format and had to find a solution that would allow it to build nationwide coverage.

But, by breaking customer comprises, CarMax has been remarkably successful. The company is profitable. On 2002 sales of $3.9 billion, they earned $94.8 million, after deducting the costs of expansion. This exceeds the average of NADA dealers. CarMax has achieved overall growth of 12 percent per year and, for comp stores, 8 percent per year. "In our first year, we did about $20 million in sales," said Austin Ligon. "This year (2003), we'll do about $4.8 billion. That's about a 24,000 percent increase. We went from about a one hundred people to nine thousand people." In its latest announcement (July 31, 2003) CarMax says it plans to add forty-four stores to its base of eighteen, and double sales to $8 billion by 2007.

The breaking of the used car buying compromise has released tremendous value, as breaking compromises always does. CarMax has created over $1 billion in value for the shareholders who received shares when CarMax was spun off from Circuit City in 2002.

HOW TO FIND COMPROMISES IN NEED OF BREAKING

The search for compromises is greatly aided if one understands why compromises exist. Compromises are what results when the limitless desires of customers to be satisfied collide with the constraints encountered by businesses in meeting these customer desires. Like the expanding universe, customers will always want more choice, better information, higher quality, greater convenience, and the greatest amount of self-indulgence—all delivered at the fastest speed and at the best price.

Creating barriers to meeting the ever-expanding demands of customers are the constraints (often referred to as the realities) of running the businesses. A company has a defined cost structure that is the result of its legacy assets—physical, personnel, IT—the levels of complexity it has accepted, its technical capabilities, and its culture. Because of these constraints, companies must set priorities in meeting the demands of customers. Often, the company's competitors will set the same priorities, since they have many of the same "lumps of coal" in their bags. Thus equilibrium is established between giving the customer what is wanted and not breaking the bank. And compromises are born.

There are many ways in which companies can find and exploit compromise-breaking opportunities in any industry:

Shop the way your customer shops. Because of the pressures of day-to-day operations, the executives of many companies are out of touch with their customers. They have only a rudimentary understanding of why their customers behave the way they do. Nowhere is this more so than with the Big Three automakers. These executives do not buy their vehicles the way their customers do. Their assistants buy their vehicles for them. The specs are called in, the order is rushed to the front of the line and the finished vehicle is delivered to the basement of the executive garage—tagged, insured, gassed up, and ready to go. To buy a vehicle the way their customers are forced to buy a vehicle would be an out-of-body experience for these executives. They need to be customers and experience the archaic form of retailing they and their dealers provide.

Know how your product or service is really bought and used. In all industries, customers devise ways of buying and using products and services so they get what they really want, which is not necessarily what the company offers. Hidden in such compensatory behaviors are compromises waiting to be broken. For example, more than 85 percent of new vehicle sales are cars bought from the dealer's inventory on the lot, rather than through a custom order or from other dealers' inventories. The manufacturers and dealers consider this to be normal customer behavior. But deeper investigation reveals that at least half of these sales are made because customers don't have the patience to wait for the vehicle they really want, or don't think the dealer will get it right even if they did wait.

The analysis also shows that when customers do order a special vehicle, they buy more options than are usually available in stock vehicles. The price for a special-order car is about 10 percent higher than a vehicle sold off the lot; for a light truck, the price is 15 percent higher. In one survey, more than half of the potential customers said they would definitely buy a car if they could specify what they wanted, pay a set price, and take delivery within two weeks. If the dealers and manufacturers could break the new car buying compromise (as Car-Max has broken the used car buying compromise) their profits would soar.

Try to make a change to your product/service delivery mechanism. Ford is regarded as having one of the best marketing and sales organizations in the auto industry. When Ford contemplated introducing the "ten day car"—a ten-day delivery on special-order vehicles—they discovered something surprising. Their marketing and sales organization is really good at "moving the metal" so the factories are busy and dealers are always loaded with vehicles. They know how to entice dealers to order what Ford can make, but they have no expertise in managing special orders for vehicles that customers want. That would require a major change in the organization, in job skills, and in activities, and would probably require a significant shift in staffing. Redesigning the organization presents a difficult and potentially painful challenge, yet the size of the prize is so large that some company, if not Ford, will step up to it. Toyota and Honda in Japan and Peugeot in France are already working on it.

Create new ways for your product/service and its delivery system to create value for customers. GM established Saturn in 1985 to serve as a laboratory for the entire organization to learn more about the business of designing, manufacturing, marketing, selling, and servicing of small cars. Saturn's family of vehicles is small in number, with reasonable quality, but mediocre performance. Its dealers are few and far between and thus not particularly convenient for buying and service. Yet, in 1994, fifty thousand Saturn owners visited the Saturn manufacturing facility in Spring Hill, Tennessee to celebrate the car. What gives?

Saturn dramatically changed the car buying experience of its customers in ways few people thought possible, by creating a no-haggle, low-pressure sales process that placed the emphasis on the wants of the customer, rather than on the needs of the manufacturer. Young women, in particular, responded positively to a process that did not require them to care about horsepower or acceleration. This is an accomplishment not to be underestimated. How did Saturn do it?

Behind the obvious elements of the story—the new facilities, sales counselors, and friendly attitude—there is a sales and manufacturing process to be admired. When a customer walks into a Saturn dealership she is given a menu of choices—body style, engine size, transmission type, color, trim, and options such as air conditioning and sound systems—with a price for each combination. When she has made her choices, the sales counselor checks to see if that vehicle is on the lot. If it isn't, they visit the sales manager. He smiles and checks his order sheet. If the customer is willing to wait thirty days, the dealer can change the engine and transmission, but not the body style, of an existing order. If there is a standing order for the body style, engine, and transmission type she wants, and only the color needs to be changed, she will have to wait only two weeks. If there is an existing order for a vehicle with all the fundamentals she wants, she can get a car with all the options she wants within a week.

Voilà! She has the car she really wants, pretty close to when she wants it.

From the time she orders the car, the customer becomes a member of the Saturn family, albeit a member in cyberspace. Saturn computers keep track of her history with the vehicle. When she sells the car, its history is transferred to the new owner—sans her name—and the family tree is extended.

This demonstrates the power of thinking in terms of customer compromises and breaking them. This is a totally new buying experience—no matter what the category—for the customer. Few potential Saturn customers were able to describe this as their ideal experience before the fact. The experience is so comforting and reinforcing that customers will often settle for an inferior vehicle rather than put themselves through the traditional process for a better car.

Saturn has created a competitive advantage that its competitors might consider unfair and that would be very difficult for them to match. "Saturn is a startup, so they can do things differently," they say. Or, "Their product offering is narrow and offers very few options." Or "They appeal to a less sophisticated buyer." Or "Saturn will lose its customers when they want to trade up in size." Yammer, yammer. Most, or all, of these excuses could be overcome by Saturn's competitors if they had the will to do so. But they don't, so Saturn has never had to face effective retaliation from a competitor.

Test the limits of your imagination. What could you do to free customers from the tyranny of your industry? How many compromises could you break? Can you find a compromise to break that could result in a radical change to your industry?

Consider household appliances. For decades, Whirlpool, the consumer appliance company, had competed against companies such as General Electric, mostly on price. In 1992, the company wanted to pursue a more profitable strategy based on a much sharper differentiation of their brand. Dave Whitwam, CEO of Whirlpool, asked his management team to specify and value all the compromises imposed by the appliance industry on its customers.

Many members of the team were skeptical, and with good reason—Whirlpool's extensive market research showed that customers were generally satisfied with the home appliances they owned. So why should they go looking for compromises that customers didn't notice or care about?

Whitwam asked them to dig deeper and, sure enough, they discovered a reservoir of suppressed dissatisfactions. Customers felt they were spending too much time and effort on the activities that appliances were supposed to make easy—laundry, food preparation, cleaning up after meals. Sure, it might take thirty minutes to cook a meal, but they still spent an hour preparing and cleaning up. Customers said they didn't expect a whole lot more from their washing machines, stoves, and dishwashers. But they were dissatisfied with the chores they had to do with them. They felt stuck in compromises, although they couldn't actually define them.

To get the Whirlpool organization to act, Whitwam knew he needed to articulate the new strategy clearly and make it real for his organization. He started by showing his management team a video clip taken from a television program on the lives of two-income families. The clip featured "Gail."

Gail was a forty-year-old woman with several children at home, a working husband, and a full-time job. She did all the cooking, laundry, and housework. Her husband's role at home was to play with the kids and to help them with their homework. At the end of the video segment the interviewer turns to Gail, who is sitting next to her beaming husband, and asks, "You're taking care of everyone in this family. Who takes care of you?" Before Gail can answer, hubby shoots back, "I take care of Gail." Gail gives him a look that could kill and starts to cry.

Gail became a rallying figure at Whirlpool and a poster child for their new strategy. Whitwam challenged all his people to think about how Whirlpool could take care of Gail. Why, for example, did it take so long for Gail to clean up after meal preparation? One reason, they decided, was that the traditional stove top had too many nooks and crannies. It had obviously been designed for simplicity of manufacture, rather than for ease of cleaning. The consumer faced a compromise: if she wanted a clean kitchen she had to put in the time wiping surfaces and digging bits of food out of crevices. To take care of Gail, Whirlpool introduced the Clean Top stove. The cooking surface is completely flat, with electric burners embedded in a glass panel, eliminating all the spatter and grease traps of the traditional designs. Another example: why did the dishwasher have to be so loud? Gail had her computer in the kitchen, but couldn't work on it when the dishwasher was running, the noise was so deafening. Nor could she talk on the phone. Whirlpool brought out the Quiet Partner dishwasher, so quiet that Gail could think and talk while it was running.

How about the auto industry? Many people are casual users of vehicles, but they have to own and operate a vehicle, with all the attendant headaches, to be assured they have a car available when they need it. There is probably a sizeable group of people who only want to drive a small number of miles each year. Could Ford offer a Gold Card program that buys the customer 2,500 miles of vehicle use each year? The customer could get a vehicle at any Hertz rental outlet. Ford would own, insure, and maintain the vehicles. Customers would get all the joys and convenience of vehicle ownership with few of the hassles.

While imagining the possibilities inherent in breaking compromises, you should also spend some time imagining the potential risks and downfalls. Sometimes it is hard to determine if the market will reward your efforts. For example, Ford would have a difficult time determining whether a Gold Card program would appeal to one thousand or one hundred thousand customers. If you can quantify the economics of the new approach, and they are attractive, the risk is probably worth taking. If you can't quantify the economics, or they look marginal, it may be wise to conduct a pilot.

Of course there are risks involved in a pilot, too. The biggest one is that you will alert your competitors. This was a problem for CarMax when it opened its store in the suburbs of Richmond, Virginia—there was no way to hide a fifteen-acre facility. So, if you do a pilot, try to run it in an out-of-the-way geography. London, Ontario, and Edmonton, Alberta, are good choices. Virtually no one in the United States pays attention to what happens there. The Japanese have begun many of their forays into the U.S. market in these cities, including Hino's cab-over-engine trucks and Matsushita's multidoor refrigerators.

Relentlessly pursue the breaking of key compromises. Speed of execution is always key to winning with a new strategy. When the strategy is based on breaking industrywide compromises, speed of execution becomes the ultimate differentiator.

Breaking compromises is a powerful organizing principle to motivate people to find major growth opportunities. If you can break one compromise, you may create a competitive advantage. If you roll out the concept rapidly enough, you can create decisive advantage.

If you can break several compromises at once and roll them out quickly, you may revolutionize your industry and become an icon.

EIGHT

Hardball M&A

Despite their high failure rate, mergers and acquisitions can be a powerful means of pursuing a hardball strategy much faster, or on a much larger scale, than could be done organically. Mergers made without a strategic rationale and acquisitions pursued on the whim of the CEO are softball moves. A good M&A deal creates competitive advantage; a great deal can help a company achieve decisive advantage, enabling it to lock up critical assets or build superior economics, making the company (almost) untouchable.

Mergers and acquisitions can be used to further any of the hardball strategies we discuss in this book. There are many other purposes of mergers and acquisitions, of course, that overlap and intertwine with these hardball strategies. Companies often pursue M&A activity to rapidly expand, nationally or globally, or annex a rival and reduce competition. There can be so much strategic benefit in merging or acquiring companies that some hardball players become serial acquirers.

There is a danger, however, in such continuous M&A activity. It can appear to be a strategy, when, in fact, it is only a tool to be used in support of a strategy. M&A as a strategy unto itself does not necessarily create competitive advantage or lead to competitive leadership. Too often, serial acquisition becomes a game, a way to gain the appearance of growth, hike share price, exploit tax loopholes, chase nonexistent synergies, gain political or social favor, settle a personal score for the CEO, or avoid fixing chronic or fundamental problems in the acquiring companies. The house built on a stack of unrelated or non-strategic acquisitions will eventually topple.

Hardball serial acquirers—such as Partners Healthcare, Cisco, Newell, and Premdor (now Masonite International)—have a clear idea of how to build competitive advantage, and have the capabilities to consummate deals and digest acquisitions for maximum strategic benefit. Companies often begin their M&A activity as a way to pursue a modest strategic goal, but end up achieving decisive advantage.

PARTNERS HEALTHCARE: A MERGER OF COMPETITORS CREATES DECISIVE ADVANTAGE

In 1994, Brigham and Women's Hospital and Massachusetts General Hospital merged to create the largest provider of health care in New England, renamed Partners HealthCare. The move surprised many of their competitors, members of the press, and business observers.

The initial idea for the merger was to cut costs and put pressure on weaker competitors, both of which are useful goals but neither of which is a strategy. The merger soon led, however, to a series of acquisitions designed to create a company with sufficient resources to attack competitors with overwhelming force, and, in the process, gain great competitive advantage and redefine the Massachusetts healthcare market.

In the early 1990s, the Boston area had an overcapacity of hospital beds. There were 5.82 beds per thousand residents, the third highest among major markets in the United States, after New York and Philadelphia. Part of the overcapacity was caused by the decrease in the length of the average patient stay. Thanks to advances in drugs and procedures, and a shift to outpatient treatment for a number of ailments, patients were admitted to the hospital less often and, when admitted, stayed for fewer days than before. Over the previous ten years, utilization rates had fallen by 30 percent, causing the cost-per-bed to rise.

To make matters worse for hospitals, health maintenance organizations (HMOs) had become extremely powerful in New England, gaining about a 35 percent share of the healthcare market. As a result, hospitals were regularly required to bid for the HMO business, often cutting prices to win it. This led to a decrease in revenues, which, combined with the rising cost per bed, put financial pressure even on the healthiest of hospitals.

Many Massachusetts hospitals struggled to survive. By the early 1990s, 40 percent of them were operating in the red, up from 20 percent the year before. Sixty-six acute care hospitals were achieving an operating margin of just 1.4 percent. Hospitals scrambled to cut costs and trim capacity. Even so, fears mounted that some of them would end up in bankruptcy.

Although Massachusetts General and Brigham and Women's were the region's largest and financially strongest hospitals, they were not immune to these worrisome trends. Both hospitals had been forced to cut their prices in order to win HMO business. They faced increased competition from suburban hospitals, which had grown larger and added capabilities that used to be available only at the big city centers. If things continued as they were, the big hospitals might be forced to reduce capacity, accept reduced revenues, cut back on services, and lose even more patients and even more revenues.

John McArthur, then the chairman of Brigham and Women's board of directors and also dean of the Harvard Business School, did not relish the idea of his hospital engaging in a price war with the HMOs and battling for every patient it could get. Instead, he considered a merger. If Brigham and Women's merged with another strong hospital, they might together have enough power and resource to improve their bargaining position with the HMOs, substantially cut costs, offer more capabilities and treatments, and, ultimately, improve their financial performance.

But McArthur and the board envisioned more than just a larger and more efficient hospital; he saw the merger as a way to fundamentally redefine the business in a way that would create competitive advantage for his hospital. "If we're just sitting here with two merged hospitals five years from now, that wouldn't be much of an achievement," McArthur told *The Boston Globe* when the merger was announced.[1]

The new Partners HealthCare started life as a formidable organization with considerable resources. It employed eighteen thousand people, including some twelve thousand doctors and nurses. The new hospital organization had more beds than any of its competitors. It had many opportunities to reduce costs by streamlining processes, combining and centralizing functions, and rationalizing facilities and activities.

Partners projected that it would cut costs by as much as 20 percent within ten years. In some industries, this might seem like a modest target, but in the healthcare industry, where costs are rapidly increasing and not entirely within the hospital's control, a 20 percent reduction sounded ambitious.

More important, the capabilities of the two prestigious hospitals, in combination, created a new organization with much greater scope. Partners became the highest-quality provider in a wide variety of specialties, making it more attractive to more patients. The size, potential cost advantage, and scope of Partners HealthCare gave the new organization, as it had hoped, significantly more power in seeking and negotiating contracts with HMOs and other insurance companies. The almost immediate result was that Partners enjoyed a larger market share than its competitors and higher bed utilization.

The combination brought other, less obvious, benefits, as well. Because of the depth of its research capabilities and with a very large pool of patients available to participate in clinical trials, Partners would be more able to compete successfully for medical research contracts, both from the federal government and private companies. As a leader in medical research, Partners would become even more attractive to patients and payers.[2]

The new organization also had sufficient resources and clout to consider making additional acquisitions. It went on to bring smaller hospitals and nursing homes into the organization, and to form joint ventures and partnerships with other powerful institutions.

Partners HealthCare had successfully created a major force in the Massachusetts healthcare industry, thanks to several reinforcing competitive advantages: higher capacity utilization and lower costs of serving patients (economies of scale); the broadest and deepest capability to support clinical research (economies of scope); and solid earnings and a stronger balance sheet (lower cost of capital), which allowed it to reinvest in its business and build its advantages even more.

The strategy forced other healthcare providers to consolidate and form alliances. But Partners had already captured many of its competitors' patients. It was ahead in cutting costs and attracting research funding. It had led the way in reducing the power of the HMOs and insurance companies. None of the competing systems is comparable to

Partners in size and scope, and they have been struggling. Partners has continued to expand its market share and increase its financial strength.

The strategy also enabled the two original entities, Brigham and Women's and Mass General, to escape the dreary fate that befalls so many players in industries that suffer from fragmentation, overcapacity, and limited market power. As we have seen in such industries as steel, major appliances, rubber and tires, airlines, PC assembly, and paper manufacturing, the players find themselves trapped in a cycle of cost cutting and consolidation. It is very difficult for any player to create competitive advantage or to gather enough force to change the dynamics of the industry.

CISCO ACQUIRES CAPABILITY IN SUPPORT OF MULTIPLE STRATEGIES

Sometimes a company does not possess a capability it needs to pursue a hardball strategy and decides to acquire it rather than try to develop it internally. One of the richest examples of an accomplished hardball player that uses M&A to acquire capability is Cisco Systems.[3]

Cisco was founded in 1984 as a provider of data routers but, early on, made a decision that enabled it to quickly become a major player in data networking. Cisco decided that it would purchase any capability it needed and that it could not quickly develop internally. Cisco became expert at the process, acquiring and integrating eighty-two companies (and shutting down a few that didn't work out), and dramatically expanding its business. Each of the acquisitions was undertaken to support a strategy (including many of the hardball strategies in this book) that would strengthen Cisco's competitive advantage.

Cisco has been successful at hardball M&A for several reasons:

- *The thoroughness of its search.* Cisco generally considers three potential markets for each one it enters and thoroughly assesses five to ten candidates for every deal it consummates.

- *The expertise and skill of its M&A team.* In pursuing deals, Cisco relies on a team composed of a small number of M&A experts, supplemented when necessary by people with needed skills who come from inside Cisco or from outside consultants or partners.

Having a group of people who are used to working with each other, under what can be highly stressful conditions, provides consistency and builds competence. And because the team works full time on M&A, they are usually able to spot opportunities and deals before the investment bankers or their rivals do.

- *The speed with which it executes deals.* A typical deal takes Cisco three months to negotiate. One senior executive joked that it takes longer to print out the purchase agreements than to negotiate them.

- *The intensity of its efforts to integrate its acquisition*s. Cisco has a dedicated integration staff to integrate IT systems, sort out the roles of new employees, make changes to compensation to retain key employees, and meet with major customers in the three months following the consummation of an acquisition.

- *Its willingness to "cut bait."* Cisco behaves like a venture capitalist, except that, unlike most VCs, Cisco takes a majority ownership position in the companies it acquires. Just like a venture capital firm, it accepts that some deals will be big winners, some will be okay, and some will be dogs. Cisco manages its portfolio of acquisitions as dispassionately and rationally as possible. It will quickly dump an acquisition or terminate an operation that does not help create or build competitive advantage.

Although we've said that M&A is not in itself a strategy, skill at M&A can be a competitive advantage. Cisco has used its ability to identify, close deals with, and integrate companies to build worldwide leadership in computer networking.

NEWELL: USING ACQUISITION TO BREAK A COMPROMISE FOR BIG BOX RETAILERS

In some cases, a company may engage in a merger or acquisition in order to create a new entity that can break a compromise that customers are being forced to tolerate. One such company is Newell Rubbermaid (formerly Newell), which began business in 1902 as a manufacturer of curtain rods, and is now the manufacturer of a variety of consumer products.[4]

From its earliest years, Newell had sold its products to large retailers such as F.W. Woolworth, Sears, and W.T. Grant. Allan Newell, the company's leader, gradually focused his company's efforts on manufacturing a limited variety of goods, at low cost, for sale to high-volume purchasers.

Dan Ferguson became president and CEO of Newell in the mid-1960s, and he realized that, as retailing consolidated and the big retailers got even bigger, the small manufacturers like Newell wouldn't be able to survive against the major manufacturers. Ferguson decided that Newell had to grow to survive. And to grow, he decided that Newell would have to offer a much wider variety of products. Ferguson decided the best way to do that was through acquisitions.

Just as Ferguson had expected, the big box retailers—including Kmart, Wal-Mart, and The Home Depot—emerged as a major force in retailing in the 1970s and 1980s. These big box retailers, for all their clout in the market, faced a compromise. In order to deliver the huge variety of low-cost goods that their consumers wanted, they had to purchase from a large number of fairly small suppliers. This complicated their logistics management and made it difficult from them to control costs. Plus, the quality of the products they were buying, in some categories, was inconsistent and the range of products from a supplier often had gaps. But when a retailer identified a quality problem or sought to improve the product line, the supplier was often unable or unwilling to respond to the retailer's needs.

Ferguson believed he could break this compromise for his customers. By increasing his pace of acquisition, he intended to make Newell into a supplier that was large enough to offer a range of products in the problem categories, disciplined enough to control and keep costs low, sophisticated enough to simplify purchasing and logistics processes, and that had enough scope to provide service nationwide.

Since the late 1960s, Newell has made more than one hundred acquisitions. Until the mid- to late 1980s, most were small companies, with sales of $5 million to $15 million, that made hardware and household products. They included EZ Paintr, a manufacturer of paint rollers and brushes; BernzOmatic, a producer of hand torches; and Mirro, a maker of cookware.

Newell became skilled at identifying the right companies to buy, and developed a set of criteria the proposed acquisition had to meet. The target company had to be large enough to be worth the investment, but not so large that it would be difficult to manage and improve. The company had to be a supplier that already had good relationships with the big retailers. The company had to be reasonably well managed; Newell was not interested in rescuing desperate companies.

As it gained experience with acquisition, Newell also got very good at integrating its newly acquired companies in a process that came to be known as Newellization. This process included a number of standard steps. The factories would be rationalized and made as efficient as possible. Service and delivery systems would be improved. Often, important personnel, particularly the CFO, would be replaced. Many services and functions would be removed from the new company and supplied by the Newell central office. The acquired company's product line would be analyzed. Poor performers would be removed. Gaps would be filled. Finally, if there were problems, a Newell executive would step in to help. "If an acquisition gets into trouble," said Ferguson, "the guy who wanted to do the deal is sent in to fix it. Sometimes that's me!"

Newell's acquisition strategy did break the big retailers' purchasing compromise, and its revenues soared: from under $20 million in the late 1960s, to $138.5 million in 1980, to more than $2 billion in the mid-1990s. Its profits also increased dramatically. Total returns to shareholders were among the highest of any company listed on the NYSE and were nearly 150 times the market average.

As Newell grew, the size of its acquisitions grew, as well. In 1987, the company paid $340 million to buy Anchor Hocking, whose sales of about $760 million were nearly twice those of Newell. Then, in 1998, Newell set its sights on a much, much bigger acquisition target: Rubbermaid. Selling price: $6 billion.

Rubbermaid did not meet Newell's own criteria for an attractive acquisition candidate. Most important, it was too large to be easily understood and managed. In 1998, Newell had revenues of $3.7 billion, not vastly greater than Rubbermaid's $2.5 billion in sales. It would not be easy for Newell to step in and fix Rubbermaid if something went wrong.

Nor did Rubbermaid have good relationships with its retail customers. In fact, it had alienated many of them. Rubbermaid, like many other big suppliers, had been slow to accept that the balance of power had shifted from supplier to retailer.

Rubbermaid had long followed a strategy known as "a new product a day" and was used to having enough clout to require its customers to carry a large range of its products. But the discount retailers didn't want to take the whole Rubbermaid line. They didn't want to carry the innovative new products that had yet to build a customer base, nor did they want to keep older, low-volume sellers on the shelves. They wanted only the fast movers.

Rubbermaid was also unhelpful to the retailers in their efforts to increase supply chain efficiencies. When retailers placed a large order for several different products made by a single supplier, they expected the order to show up in one shipment. But Rubbermaid had traditionally shipped products direct from their dozens of factories. A big order from Rubbermaid would arrive in many smaller shipments, at different times. That's if they showed up at all—Rubbermaid had a dismal on-time delivery record.

Finally, Rubbermaid was not accustomed to the intense price pressure they now got from the big retailers. Rubbermaid's product line was based on plastic resin, a commodity whose price was volatile. In the past, Rubbermaid had been able to pass along the price increases to their retailers. But retailers had become increasingly unwilling to pay.

As a result of these difficulties in dealing with Rubbermaid, some retailers—Wal-Mart among them—reduced the number of Rubbermaid products they carried.

The Newellization of Rubbermaid continues to this day. Product lines are being focused. Factories are being revamped. Underperforming businesses are being divested. Marketing programs to placate big customers are in place. Revenues from large retailers have stopped declining and are beginning to grow. The Newell portfolio continues to expand and includes many well-known brands, including Papermate, Sharpie, and Waterman writing implements; Levolor window blinds;

Calphalon cookware; BernzOmatic propane torches; Vise-Grip pliers; Amerock hardware; Graco baby gear; and Little Tikes toys.

But the Rubbermaid experience was bad enough that investors are still wary.

MASONITE INTERNATIONAL: ACQUISITIONS FOR GLOBAL GROWTH

Acquisition has been the preferred mode of international expansion for most U.S. and European companies since World War II. Such companies generally sought to expand by acquiring companies that were in the same or a related business and operating in a market that looked attractive.

More often than not, this approach has resulted in a global business that is a string of pearls: a portfolio of locally managed investments whose managers enjoy considerable autonomy as long as they make their numbers. The parent company rarely intervenes, except to supply capital when needed, and to hire, fire, or move a manager.

A sharp contrast to this approach is the competitor who moves into foreign markets not just for growth but also to create and exploit two sources of competitive advantage. The first is the leveraging of investments across a global business base. These can be investments in product and production technologies but may also include information systems and management practices, such as a uniform "face to the customer" that has proven to be successful. These investments may be of a scale so large that local competitors can't match them utilizing the resources that are available only from their local operations.

Another form of investment lies in portfolio management. This is particularly true for businesses that require considerable investments in expense-related items to grow. A competitor with a portfolio of operations around the world is in an advantaged positioned relative to a local competitor. He can take money made in one, secure locale, and invest it in an emerging market, and he can do so at a rate greater than the indigenous competitor might be able to do. Too bad for the indigenous competitor.

The second source of competitive advantage comes from being in the markets where potential global competitors may be. These are the markets of companies that might be tempted to come into your home markets. You are in a much better position to influence their behavior by being in their home markets than when they show up down the street.

A great example of a company competing globally beyond just managing a "string of pearls" is Masonite International, based in Mississauga, Ontario. The company is one of the world's largest manufacturers of doors and door components, such as frames, glass inserts, lights, panels, and weather stripping.

Masonite International has a complicated genealogy. It had been a business unit of Seaway Multicorp, a family-held conglomerate in Canada, and was spun off as Premium Forest Products in a leveraged buyout in 1979. The company went public in 1986, at which time it changed its name to Premdor. It did not become known as Masonite International until 2001, when it acquired its largest supplier, Masonite, the manufacturer of wood-composite products.

The Canadian door industry of the 1970s and 1980s, in which Premdor, as Masonite International was then known, was fragmented. Many small players, each offering a limited line of products, fought fiercely for business. Although small, they often had trouble fully utilizing the capacity of their factories. And, as a result of the U.S.-Canadian free trade agreement, the Canadian companies increasingly found themselves competing with U.S.-based companies.

Saul M. Spears, who had headed the company through its LBO and then its public offering, aggressively acquired companies through the 1980s. Most of them were based in Canada but some of them were based in the United States. His goal was to consolidate the industry in Canada and discourage U.S. companies from attacking his Canadian markets. His crowning achievement was the 1989 merger with his major Canadian competitor, Century Wood Door, which had been pursuing a similar strategy and had a sizable U.S. operation. The deal instantly transformed Premdor into one of the biggest door companies in the world, with sales of more than CND 300 million. Besides heading off a potentially destructive battle with Century in Canada, the merger promised to give Premdor the scale and market position it needed to counter the American threat. Spears said at the time, "If American competitors find their domestic market under attack, they will be less likely to bother with new Canadian markets."[5]

Philip S. Orsino, who had been Century's president, became CEO of the combined companies, which retained the name Premdor. Orsino continued the strategy of growth by acquisition, purchasing more companies in the United States and then in Europe and Mexico. The market dynamics that Premdor had exploited in Canada also existed in rest of world. In most countries, the markets were localized and fragmented. There were only a few big companies making doors for the worldwide market, but they were diversified building products manufacturers with no great interest in building their door businesses.

Such conditions create an opportunity for a hardball competitor to achieve decisive advantage. If it can achieve economies of scale (in its purchasing of materials or components, for example), make investments in product development and service that rivals can't match, and quickly migrate best practices—such as fast equipment changeover—from one company to another, it may be able to gain a powerful advantage over its smaller, local competitors.

There were other benefits to acquiring local companies. In many markets there was already too much manufacturing capacity; building a new plant would have added more. Plus, Premdor chose to buy companies that had good relationships with their customers—building products wholesalers and retailers—that would otherwise be difficult, and would take time, to build.

In the twenty-five years since it began operating independently, the company has grown from a small producer of interior residential wood doors into a global giant. It has more than seventy facilities in twelve countries in North America, South America, Europe, Asia, and Africa, revenues of nearly $1.78 billion and $108 million in net income, and sells its products in more than fifty countries. Along the way, the company has completed forty acquisitions, each designed to strengthen its competitive advantage in a specific way.

In 1998, for example, Premdor purchased the door fabrication operations of Georgia-Pacific. The acquisition enabled Premdor to launch a network of logistical and fabrication centers to serve the big box home improvement chains in the United States such as The Home Depot and Lowe's. The centers provide a variety of services, including hanging doors in frames, machining doors for hinges and locksets, and inserting decorative glass panes. Premdor had already been successful in capitalizing on the preference of these chains to deal with a big, full-line supplier, rather than a slew of small suppliers with narrow product lines.[6]

In 2001, Premdor purchased Masonite for $437 million, and the new entity became Masonite International. The acquisition brought a powerful brand into the family as well as a host of other advantages. The original Masonite was a global manufacturer of door facings, and a leader in the design and technology of the wood composites they are made from. The deal strengthened the combined company's ability to create unique designs for different markets around the world and get the designs to its markets faster. This is because the door facings, unlike entire door assemblies, can be produced in high volumes and economically shipped to local markets, either directly to a Masonite International facility in markets where the company was already established, or to a local producer in markets where Masonite International had yet to establish a presence. And, because molded doors are less expensive to manufacture than many other kinds of doors, they can be sold at a lower price.

In 2004, Masonite International acquired the entry door business of Stanley Works for $160 million. Masonite International's main strength has always been in interior doors, and it still is. But Stanley Works makes steel and fiberglass entry doors, and its acquisition has enabled Masonite International to expand its offering of exterior doors. The deal also helped Masonite International move into "entry systems"— doors pre-hung in a frame. To compete in these products requires technology and capital that indigenous competitors in local markets may not have. This creates an opportunity for Masonite International to develop further advantage by migrating its systems capability to its operations around the globe.

Over the years, Masonite International has become adept at making acquisitions that will further its strategy and build its competitive advantage. Before it acquires a company, Masonite International takes pains to develop a close working relationship with the prospect—by taking a financial stake in it or forming an alliance of some kind. This allows Masonite International to make sure it knows what it is buying, and accelerate the integration once the deal has closed.

When Masonite International makes an acquisition, it immediately takes charge of the sales and marketing activities of its new family member. It has long been known for its skill in marketing directly to consumers in order to fuel demand for its doors at the big home improvement centers, as well as at wholesale and retail lumber yards, and building supply centers. In addition, Masonite International brings the new company into its computer network, installs its financial control systems, centralizes purchasing, improves production techniques, and integrates the new company's factories into its regional manufacturing network.[7]

Masonite International is succeeding in consolidating the industry through its acquisition activity. There are still many small, local producers of door products, and there are still large diversified building products companies against whom Masonite International competes. But Masonite International has only one major global rival—JELD-WEN, a privately held company based in Oregon.

Consolidation by acquisition has been very good to Masonite International, which has enjoyed expanding margins, rapid sales growth, and increasing market share over the past decade.

HOW TO WIN AT HARDBALL M&A

Hardball players apply focus, speed, and intensity to all stages of M&A. They are better at identifying the specific asset or capability needed to achieve competitive advantage and deciding whether it's best to develop it internally or obtain it externally. They excel in identifying and assessing targets, calculating the maximum price to be paid, negotiating deals fast in a disciplined fashion (and walking away if a deal gets too pricey), and then integrating acquisitions quickly and efficiently in order to achieve the strategic objectives. They know what they want and then get it at a price that's in line with the acquisition's strategic value.

The lessons from serial acquirers that use M&A to carry out their hardball strategies are straightforward in concept but difficult to execute:

- *Acquire only if the opportunity fits with the strategy.* Mergers and acquisitions should be pursued only if they will help you attain or strengthen competitive advantage. They should not be played as a game, or pursued as a way to meet interesting new people, take factory tours, and gain bragging rights.

- *Do not be tempted to step outside your proven process.* When the business model based on acquisitions works, especially when it has continued to work through a series of acquisitions, be wary of deviating from it. After successfully acquiring and integrating many companies, Newell was confident that it could take on a bigger challenge. But Rubbermaid did not meet the criteria that had made Newell's earlier acquisitions so successful. Even the vaunted Newellization process broke down.

- *If you're going to change the acquisition criteria, you may need to change the acquisition process, too.* Newell, for example, might have considered bringing in executives skilled in turnaround. They might have structured the acquisition to keep it at arm's length from Newell's successful core. They might have structured the deal differently. Or they might have walked away from Rubbermaid when they realized how difficult it would be to integrate the company into their system.

- *Build an internal M&A capability.* Many a CEO has lived to regret succumbing to the unsolicited pitches of investment bankers. Companies that are contemplating a major acquisition, or a series of acquisitions or mergers, should develop their own M&A capability, building a team that can generate M&A ideas, explore and analyze them, do their own due diligence, and negotiate the deals.

- *Seek outside advice and assistance.* Even with a capable internal M&A capability, companies contemplating an acquisition can often benefit from the assistance of outside experts in a particular industry or business area, or from the counsel of an adviser who does not stand to directly gain from the acquisition. Such outside advisers should be used to increase the knowledge and skill of the acquirer, and provide a perspective on the acquisition that is free of traditional industry assumptions and unbiased by internal politics. Most important, the outside adviser should be able to help identify the sources of competitive advantage to be exploited by the merger or acquisition and the best path to obtaining that advantage. How many CEOs do their own brain surgery, close their own real estate deals, or manage their own divorces without the aid of outside advisers?

- *Take a rigorous approach to valuation.* When assessing the value of a proposed acquisition, it is necessary to analyze how the purchase will affect the value of your company, as well as how much it is worth on the open market. For example, will the acquisition rob resources from other of your initiatives? If you forfeit the acquisition to a competitor, how might it strengthen that rival? Or, can an acquisition be "lost" in a way that hurts your rival? How do your customers and suppliers view the acquisition? How will it change your industry? How, exactly, will the acquisition benefit your company? How might it cause trouble? How will integration be accomplished, by whom, and how much will it cost?

- *Invest in post merger integration (PMI) capability so you have the capacity to successfully integrate acquisitions.* The majority of mergers and acquisitions don't work as well as the participants had hoped. Some are outright disasters. Some, like Newell's acquisition of Rubbermaid, take longer and cost much more than expected. Many of them would have been more successful if the integration process had been better managed. Too many executives think that once the deal is done and the integration plan has been written, the acquisition is over. But integration can be the most difficult part, and it's where many deals fall apart.

NINE

Changes in the Field of Play

The strategies we have outlined in this book are classics, but "classic" should not be interpreted to mean "static." The game of hardball is dynamic and always evolving. New barriers to achieving competitive advantage emerge and new roadblocks to building decisive advantage are erected. There are issues that are so significant and complex (like the rising power of China) that they become chronic, and can never completely be removed from the managerial agenda.

In this chapter, we outline several issues that will affect the way the game of hardball must be played in the future and that change the rules for players who wish to be winners, especially on the global field.

PLAYING THE CHINA CARD

China will be the biggest and most contentious issue in the next decade for hardball players, even if they are not global companies themselves. China will be the source of tough competitors, and as thorny an issue for all companies as Japan was in the 1980s.

But China today is different than Japan was then, and it has the potential to be even more challenging and influential in world business. As a market and a source of future competitors it is vastly bigger than

Japan, and it has come onto the scene much faster. Although governmental and commercial practices in China present barriers to Western company expansion there, as they did in Japan, Western companies can buy positions in China more readily than they could in Japan in the early post-war years. Now is the time for business leaders to recognize that they will have to play the China card or be played by it. Here's how hardball players will do so:

Drive down costs. The first move is to drive down your costs faster than your competitors can, and use the cost saving to upset their strategies. Productivity and quality-adjusted costs of Chinese factory labor are often 30 to 40 percent less than those of the United States and Europe. These differences are driving the primary effect on competition—the race is to achieve lower cost without necessarily changing strategy. These Chinese cost advantages have attracted, and will continue to attract, makers of products that have high labor content, growth potential, attractiveness to the Chinese domestic market, standard manufacturing processes, and relatively simple logistics.

There is no doubt that going to China can save costs, but whether those cost swings make it to your bottom line is entirely dependent on what your competitors do. Go earlier than your competitors and there will be bottom line improvements until your competitors follow. If they go at the same time as you do, very little of the savings will survive the price competition that is sure to follow and make it to your bottom line.

The best plan is to go to China early and use the savings you realize to fund new strategies that will help you create competitive advantage. This is what Emerson Electric did in the late 1990s and early 2000s, in order to attack Black & Decker in professional power tools. A decade earlier, Black & Decker had taken a little-known brand of power tools called DEWALT, created a full line of tools around it, and built a strong business with both contractors and consumers. But Black & Decker continued to manufacture DEWALT in the United States. Emerson Electric decided to attack DEWALT with its own brand, Ridgid, but they would source its production in China. Ridgid has grown from nothing to a position to be reckoned with in the U.S. power tool market. Black & Decker has announced a restructuring. And it is planning to transfer more of the DEWALT manufacturing to non-U.S. facilities.

Win the Chinese domestic market. The second China card to play is to win in the Chinese domestic market. Western companies are rushing to China to outsource production from their high-cost factories and suppliers at home. Many try to get equity positions in their new supplier companies, but few realize they are sowing the seeds for the growth of their suppliers, which are likely to become their competitors in the future. Western companies want to believe that when they source their whole goods from China they retain their relationships with customers, and are the ultimate owners of the brand. Not necessarily.

Take flat-screen televisions. Flat screens have penetrated the market so quickly that the experts have barely had time to comment. Traditional brands such as Philips and Sony are being pushed aside by Chinese brands and upstart western brands, such as Dell and Gateway, that are supplied by Chinese producers.

When the dust settles, the leaders will be those companies that are not just the leading suppliers to Western brands but are also the leading brands in the Chinese market itself. The Western brand companies that only source from China will find themselves in a high-cost position as buyers from their competitors. The Westerners may also find they can't touch the profit sanctuaries their Chinese competitors have secured in the domestic market.

Use the supply chain wisely. The third Chinese card to play is the greatest trade barrier of all—time. China is a long way from the United States. When U.S. companies rely on Chinese suppliers they are stretching their supply chain over the greatest possible distance the world allows. Every aspect of supply chain management, already a difficult discipline, becomes even more difficult. The stretched supply chain is very susceptible to small changes in demand that result in huge distortions along its length. The stretch also makes it difficult to identify and remove quality problems when they arise.

Bluff when you have no China card to play. Some types of products are not well-suited to creation or production within the extended supply chain, including those that depend on customer-driven innovation and those whose customers have a high sensitivity to product quality (real or perceived) and provenance. If you have developed a competitive advantage with such products in the U.S. market, and believe that your business will not benefit by playing the China card, you may be able to strengthen your advantage by influencing your competitors to source their products in China. One way to do so is to make a smart bluff. Announce your intention of moving your sourcing to China and pursue some activities that make your competitors believe it, such as starting a small pilot there or engaging a firm to look for a site on which to build a facility. Then, take your time, do just enough to convince your competitors you're serious (but not enough to actually accomplish anything or waste any resources), and watch as your competitors dash to China and muck up their businesses.

Whatever China card you decide to play, remember that the next hand is already being dealt. It's called India.

GETTING STUCK IN THE MIDDLE

During the past decade, the shift from a producer-driven economy to a consumer-driven economy in the United States has become an important issue for companies in virtually every industry and business segment. Many of them have yet to recognize it, however, or have leaders that refuse to believe it.[1]

As a result of changes in consumer demographics and behavior, in combination with changes in retailing, the market for consumer goods has become polarized. At the very high end, some luxury brands, such as Gucci and Rolls-Royce, continue to succeed by selling superexpensive goods at very high margins and in very small quantities. But there are so few consumers who can afford these goods that the brands cannot grow very much or gather the resources to change very fast. At the low end, a wide variety of brands of commodities and utilitarian items—including household and office products, food staples, home electronics, toys, and hardware—compete with each other on price and minor product differentiations. These brands, including private label or generic brands, may grow in volume but must fight ferociously to retain or grow profits.

The fastest-growing segment in the market is in premium goods that are still affordable to middle market consumers. These are goods and services, priced from 20 to 200 percent above midpriced offerings, that offer enough technical differences and performance improvements, along with emotional engagement, that consumers are willing to pay extra for them. These new luxury brands include small, low-priced items such as Aveda personal care, Grey Goose and Belvedere vodka, and Starbucks coffee. They also include more expensive items such as a Viking stove or a set of Callaway golf clubs. And they go all the way up to big-ticket purchases, such as a premium cruise or a Mercedes C-class sedan.

And then there is the middle, where no consumer or manufacturer wants to be, the territory where hundreds of companies and brands have gotten stuck, including Kmart, Jordan Marsh, Toys "R" Us, Miller, Pontiac, Healthtex, Hersheys, Kenmore, Smirnoff, Levis, Gateway, Reebok, and Swanson.

You know you're playing softball and are in danger of being stuck in the middle if:

- *Your product is undifferentiated from its competitors, but sells at a higher price than similar, widely available products.* Why buy a pair of Haggar slacks for $65 at a department store when you can buy a perfectly good pair of Gap khakis for $39?

- *Your product sells at a substantial premium based on its brand name without delivering on value, features, or emotional engagement.* Godiva is getting perilously close to this situation. The sale of the Porsche Boxster declined within two years of introduction, possibly because consumers could get just as much performance and excitement at lower prices from the Honda S2000 and other vehicles, and didn't think the Porsche name was worth the extra money.

- *Your product is mediocre in quality, design, or performance.* Only if there is absolutely no alternative will the consumer settle for a product that is poorly made, has defects, looks ugly, or performs poorly. Usually these products are ones that people have to have but won't dress up to be seen using—such as a vacuum cleaner.

- *Your product has no story or context.* Consumers of premium goods do not want to buy them from huge, anonymous companies. They want to know who the people are behind the product and they want to understand the context of the category. The Sub-Zero refrigerator has a more interesting story than an Amana. Even Dell, whose product has become a commodity, has an intriguing and accessible story behind it (starring Michael Dell, boy entrepreneur), in comparison to HP (once-great company, now faded in an awkward merger) or Gateway (something about cows).

Softball players would like to believe they can operate outside the rules of the new market. They will rely on one or more softball tactics to stave off the death that surely awaits if they don't address these vital issues. They will:

- *Count on customer loyalty.* In the face of a strong competitive challenge, they will hope their traditional customers will stick by them, for old times' sake. Some will, but not forever. Lincoln is the classic example.

- *Attract customers with sharp advertising and clever marketing.* Consumers love good advertising, and it may drive them to try a new product or to stick with an old favorite for a while longer than they might have otherwise. But hoping for advertising to pull you out of the middle is playing softball. Miller High Life has tried, and it doesn't work.

- *Replicate without starting the heartbeat.* Many companies that find themselves stuck in the middle make an attempt at copying the market leader, but fail to understand the customer experience. Dunkin' Donuts may fall into this trap in their effort to copy the Starbucks espresso-based coffee business by offering lattes and cappuccinos.

- *Ignore or explain away anomalies.* Why do some people buy groceries for their dinner every night from the small neighborhood shop where the goods are fresh but the choice is narrower and prices are higher? Could it be they are willing to pay a higher price because they want to decide what to eat at the last minute? And that they are too busy and stressed to deal with a crowded supermarket at the end of the day?

Hardball players faced with getting stuck in the middle, by contrast, learn as much as they can about the customer, decide whether they will move up or down in the market, and face up to the fact that customers are no longer loyal to undeserving brands and, most important, will move to the deserving one as soon as it appears.

Hardball players will do whatever it takes to get out of the middle.

DEALING WITH STRANDED ASSETS

A nasty side effect of gaining competitive advantage and creating a virtuous cycle that builds into decisive advantage is the stranding of assets. This happens when an asset that was once a contributor to competitive advantage becomes irrelevant or, worse, a drag on competitiveness.

The term "stranded" entered the business lexicon at the time of the deregulation of electric power businesses. Very often, the high costs of operating a power-generation asset—such as a small, oil-fired generator—have been hidden in the average pricing of a large portfolio of power-generation assets. When the portfolio is unbundled, it is revealed that the costs of operating the generating facility are higher than the prices currently being charged for its product. There are no customers willing to pay the price that would be necessary to cover costs and make the asset profitable. The original investment has not been recouped. The asset is stranded; it lingers on the balance sheet waiting for the write-down that is sure to come.

Forces such as globalization, technological change, and corporate self-interest continuously intensify competition and strand many kinds of assets, including:

- *Physical.* The list of physical stranded assets awaiting write-down includes old shopping malls, manufacturing facilities of the major automotive and appliance manufacturers, unused or under utilized square footage of department stores, and rail lines that go from nowhere to nowhere and back again.

- *People.* Many companies have people assets that are stranded. There is much teeth gnashing over high-paying jobs in the United States being moved to India. The people put out of work by such moves are stranded assets. So are the workers and retirees in the automotive and heavy manufacturing industries who are highly paid and receive significant healthcare and pension benefits.

- *Suppliers.* When the compressor manufacturer in Ohio moves production to China, the company in Indiana that supplied it with cardboard shipping cartons becomes stranded.

- *Customers.* A surprising number of companies are finding themselves with stranded customers, mostly because of the aging of the customer base. Changes in technologies and practices can also result in stranded customers. An increasing reliance on outpatient procedures and better technologies that result in shorter hospital stays are stranding a key asset: hospital beds.

Softball competitors rally around stranded assets attempting to push off the day of reckoning when the assets will have to be written off. They seek government aid. They try to push the problem onto the public, as the auto industry is trying to do with healthcare costs. The longer the delay the greater the pain will be in the long run.

Hardball competitors strive to eliminate, and when possible, re-purpose their stranded assets. If he is on his toes and gets on with the task, a retailer weighed down by uncompetitive leases can work his way out of the problem in five years. An auto manufacturer can migrate away from its antiquated dealer network in ten years if it enforces new standards whenever a dealership changes hands.

Wilbur Ross, at International Steel Group, is a hardball competitor who takes over ailing steel companies. He closes their unproductive assets. He sheds high-cost labor contracts. He shifts pension liabilities to a government agency that was created, in part, to ensure that retired union members would not lose their pensions. He offers new jobs, at lower wage rates, to workers he has fired.

Wilbur Ross is successful. The media hails him. But he doesn't particularly enjoy the work that fills his days. Why should he? He is doing the dirty work that previous softball steel executives could not muster the courage to do. If they had faced the problems earlier, the changes would have been less severe and would not have hurt as much. "Admissions of error, admission of defeat, restructuring, laying people off," Ross told *BusinessWeek*, "are not American ideals."[2]

When suppliers are in danger of being stranded, they can move to China when their customers do. Or, better yet, before their customers do. This is what Smurfit-Stone Container, a manufacturer of cardboard boxes, is doing.

Cadillac has been dealing with the stranding of customers. As early as the 1970s, both Cadillac and Lincoln faced the problems of an aging and shrinking customer base. Ford separated Lincoln from the Ford Division, moved its headquarters to California, and gave the Lincoln executives a new mandate: Become relevant to younger customers by offering entry-level luxury vehicles that are competitive with the European luxury imports. When the company suffered substantial losses in the early 2000s, Ford retreated from its bold break with the past and brought Lincoln back to Detroit and buried the brand inside its North American organization.

In contrast, GM made no organizational changes. It invested in bold, risky new product designs and higher quality in an attempt to woo new customers and revive the Cadillac customer base. Cadillac's new models have gotten a lot of media attention and are selling well enough that Cadillac is emboldened to make a stab at marketing its vehicles in Europe.

GM is playing hardball with its stranded asset.

BEING "WAL-MARTED"

The Borg is a character in the television show *Star Trek: The Next Generation,* an alien life form that is part human and part machine. A network known as "the collective" links its life forms to one another. The Borg regularly attacks alien cultures and absorbs them into the collective, saying, "Resistance is futile. You will be assimilated." The Borg is unstoppable.

Wal-Mart is the Borg of business today, the largest retailer on the planet. It is more than three times larger, when measured in sales, than the next largest retailer, Carrefour. (Carrefour has more stores.) Wal-Mart is the largest, or among the top three largest, sellers of many categories of goods, including groceries, family clothing, toys, personal care products, home electronics, magazines, and others. Wal-Mart continues to push into new categories with catastrophic consequences to traditional competitors. Its cost position is so strong that their competitors' attempts to match it on "every day low prices" end in failure. As one of our colleagues observed, "The world has never known a company with such ambition, capability, and momentum."

Wal-Mart presents a dilemma to its suppliers. It is the most profitable customer for many suppliers on an absolute basis and often on the basis of percentage. It helps everyone strip out costs from the supply chain. Although it keeps a lot of the savings, it also share some of them with its suppliers. So suppliers dearly want to keep their Wal-Mart business.

However, Wal-Mart has another agenda that is not so beneficial to their suppliers. It wants to stock your brand to build traffic to their stores, but it really wants the consumer to buy Wal-Mart's private label products once they get there, because they are far more profitable for the retailer. The fastest growing apparel brand? Wal-Mart's Faded Glory—$10 for a pair of jeans, some of which are sourced from Mexico, the same country that supplies Wrangler jeans that sell for $14.

Another big Wal-Mart threat, as Rubbermaid so painfully learned, is that when it represents such a large percentage of your business, it can hurt you badly if it dumps you. (It accounts for some 25 percent of P&G's domestic business.) So, to avoid being Wal-Marted, make sure you balance your portfolio by selling through other channels and into international markets.

But there are chinks in the monolith's armor.

Customers are forced into a compromise when they shop at Wal-Mart. They usually have to travel a long distance to get to a store. They have to park in a large, crowded lot. They must roam through acres of retail space, through aisles designed to take them ever deeper into the store. Sales help is scarce and not always knowledgeable. The prices are dramatically low, but the experience is mediocre at best and unpleasant at worst. Some customers (although probably fewer than the media would like you to believe) refuse to shop at Wal-Mart because they don't enjoy the experience. Others refuse to shop there because they are opposed to Wal-Mart's effect on communities or dislike their labor practices.

Some suppliers don't like Wal-Mart, either, and won't sell to them. They believe that Wal-Mart stifles innovation. James A. Wier, CEO of Simplicity Manufacturing, told *BusinessWeek,* "Wal-Mart really is about driving the cost of a product down." Simplicity makes lawn mowers, and made the decision to stop selling to Wal-Mart. "When you drive the cost of a product down, you really can't deliver the high-quality product like we have."[3]

Whether to sell to Wal-Mart is your choice to make. The carrot is the large volume of purchases. The stick is the need to submit to the Wal-Mart way, including pricing that is expected to always go down. The promise is that your brand will get huge exposure and increase its customer base. The danger is that your brand will lose its vibrancy in its association with Wal-Mart and that you will not have enough cash to innovate and improve the product.

Your strategy options include:

- *Don't sell to Wal-Mart at all.* Accept the fact that your sales will be lower but your margins will likely be higher, and accept the risk of your competitors selling to Wal-Mart. If they do, they will achieve higher volume than you can, drive down costs, and may then attack the profit sanctuaries you have created in alternative channels.

- *Sell some products or brands to Wal-Mart, but create a separate product line that you sell through other channels.* This will be difficult. If the outside brand is successful Wal-Mart will want that one too, and can leverage your existing sales with them to convince you to give the new brand to them, as well.

- *Establish a pattern of rapid product innovation.* Sell new products outside of Wal-Mart for as long as possible at as high a premium as possible and then sell through Wal-Mart when the products mature. But Wal-Mart is quick. The window of opportunity won't be open very long. They will likely want to bring the new products inside before you'd like them to. If you resist, they may create a knock-off, as they did with Mainstays, which is positioned against Martha Stewart's Everyday brand at Kmart.

It is very difficult to play hardball against a hardball player as accomplished as Wal-Mart. However, in addition to breaking the compromise of the customer experience, there are two other possibilities:

- *Exploit anomalies.* Even with Wal-Mart's enormous inventory, it is focused on utilitarian goods at low prices. It has not been successful in competing against premium new luxury brands of the type described earlier in this chapter. Such goods appeal strongly to groups of consumers that are, by nature, anomalous to the undifferentiated "general population" that is Wal-Mart's customer base. Most important, such premium products are sold, and very profitably, on the basis of emotional engagement—at purchase and in use. The Wal-Mart atmosphere is the antithesis of new luxury. The shopping experience does not enhance the product; it often degrades it. It costs money to create an appealing store environment, through better layout and design, lighting and fixtures— money that Wal-Mart is reluctant to spend.

Internet retailers such as Tesco and grocerygateway.com can be seen as exploiting the same anomaly—the willingness of some customers to pay higher prices for a better experience. Internet-savvy consumers who value their time and want competitive prices, but don't need the very lowest prices, find shopping online to be a perfectly acceptable substitute for shopping at Wal-Mart and other big box retailers. At grocerygateway.com, shoppers can get groceries at competitive prices, hardware from The Home Depot, liquor, and more, at the click of a mouse. The goods are delivered within an agreed-upon time and unloaded into the house. No driving. No parking. No crowds. No wandering the endless aisles. No lugging packages. No Wal-Mart.

- *Raise costs.* Wal-Mart is also vulnerable on its image. It is perceived by some people, not as a hardball player, but as a bully. Wal-Mart has taken heat for pressuring its employees to work unpaid overtime, offering meager health benefits, damaging small businesses, polluting the environment, and even for being philanthropically stingy. A smart competitor may figure out a way to raise Wal-Mart's costs by exposing Wal-Mart's performance on a specific issue, bettering that performance, and forcing Wal-Mart to raise its costs in that area. But be careful, Wal-Mart's costs are so low in comparison to their competitors it will be difficult to force them up enough to make Wal-Mart feel the pain.

Eventually, Wal-Mart's business model may no longer provide the growth it wants or needs. One potential source of trouble for Wal-Mart is global expansion. The company cannot maintain its domestic growth rate for many more years; they will have to figure out how to grow internationally, where they have struggled for years. If Wal-Mart's growth rate falls, while that of others increases, its economic model may destabilize and become vulnerable to attack. Perhaps a new kind of competitor will emerge to challenge the big box concept. A likely one is some form of online retailing that effectively provides a much larger box than the biggest bricks-and-mortar retailer could ever build, while dramatically improving the shopping experience.

Market forces may change, or new ones may emerge, that will threaten Wal-Mart's supply chain–based competitive advantage. We don't know what they will be, but they always have emerged, and—barring any government attempts to "fix" the problem—they will prevail again.

What is Wal-Mart if not the current incarnation of history's "undefeatable" human achievements? "Wal-Mart is the logical end point and the future of the economy in a society whose preeminent value is getting the best deal," Robert B. Reich, former secretary of labor, told the *New York Times*.[4] The history of warfare, however, is littered with "ultimate weapons" that eventually became obsolete. The crossbow. The battleship. The ICBM.

But even if Wal-Mart is eventually marginalized or defeated, it is likely that a different Borg will arise and present some new, seemingly insurmountable, challenge to the world's competitors.

TEN

The Hardball Mindset

To play the game of hardball to its fullest requires a hardball state of mind. In this book, we have not focused on such matters as personal coaching, skills building, or self-improvement. But, as our stories show—and as we know very well from our experience with clients—playing hardball entails more than strategy.

Hardball players possess a number of admirable characteristics. They have an intellectual toughness that enables them to face facts and see reality. They have an emotional awareness that means they know themselves, and their people, well. They are always dissatisfied with the status quo, no matter how fine things may seem, and they have the will to catalyze change. They're tough, but they're not bullies. They're serious about their business, but they also have fun playing the game. They have such an intense passion for winning that it rubs off on others.

The hardball player needs all of these qualities, and more, in order to accomplish his most important task: to get to the heart of the matter and stay there. The heart of the matter is that set of fundamental, often systemic, issues that is limiting the growth and success of the business. These issues are often so challenging in so many ways that no one in the organization has the guts to take them on or the ability to actually solve them.

Getting to the heart of the matter is not easy, and it requires doing more than just identifying what the heart of the matter is. A large consumer products company, for example, had once been hugely profitable but, in just a few years, went from making millions in profits to losing millions. Now the company is systemically broken. It is trapped in several vicious circles that make it hard to improve its cost, time, or quality performance. Japanese and German competitors are eating away at its share.

For this company, the heart-of-the-matter issues include: the need to close inefficient plants, renegotiate agreements with labor unions, eliminate certain products, and reduce the complexity of core processes. Each issue is difficult to face, difficult to create solutions for, difficult to communicate to the organization, and, above all, difficult to execute against. Management at this company cannot even bring themselves to face the issues at the heart of the matter. As a result, they remain like deer frozen in the headlights, watching in disbelief as their competitors roar toward them and prepare to run them down.

Confronting the heart of the matter and fixing the issues there, especially in fiercely competitive markets, can be physically and psychologically taxing. It is much easier to make the small, daily decisions of business-as-usual and take incremental actions than to make the tough decisions necessary in the heart of the matter. As Roger Enrico showed at Frito-Lay, living at the heart of the matter means making big moves on big things. That takes guts.

People and organizations can come up with many excuses for avoiding heart-of-the-matter issues, and they all sound plausible. Popular ones are, "That's not my problem," even when it is. Or, "We've tried to solve this problem a thousand times before," even when they've never really committed themselves to any of the initiatives designed to solve it. Or, "We're already making good progress on this," even when they're not. Or, "It's not my fault," even when it partially is. Or, "I'm waiting for some leadership," when, in fact, it's their job to provide it.

The only way to get the organization to focus on the heart of the matter is for the senior leader to define the issues, talk about them, and attack them first. Leaders who personally live in the heart of the matter have three traits in common:

- *They live at the rock face.* Living at the rock faces means being physically and personally connected to the market—to customers, consumers, competitors, and suppliers. Talk with your customers, "staple yourself to an order," visit distributors, understand your competitors' economics as well as, if not better than, they do themselves. You have to experience your customer's experience for yourself.

Softball players avoid the customer experience. Many airline executives, for example, never stand in line at the airport or fly coach. The auto executive doesn't have to buy, finance, or insure his new car. Roger Enrico, on the other hand, lived at the rock face. He liked to go to supermarkets and hand out samples of a new product to regular customers. He said it was "as close to a religious experience as one can have in business" because it was so revelatory and meaningful. Hardball players love being their own customers.

- *They have the courage to ask simple questions.* People get promoted because they get results and have deep experience. Many senior managers can't bring themselves to say "I don't know" because it seems to undercut the very reason they hold their position. This unease prevents them from discussing the simple, fundamental questions of their business. Asking a basic question like, "Who are our customers?" can seem naive. In fact, it is essential. Saying "I don't know" can lead to breakthroughs. Leaders lose their edge and value when they assume too much. When the team at Wausau saw the sales anomaly, they asked, "Why?" When they were told it was the result of a special relationship, they asked, "What's so special about it?" Only then did they discover the real cause that could be exploited into competitive advantage.

- *They build a truth-telling network.* Hardball is a team sport. You can't win by yourself, no matter how close to the rock face you live, or how courageous you are in asking simple questions. The problem is that most of the people you interact with, starting with your direct reports, won't share your hardball mindset.

Employees, operating out of self-interest, often shade the truth when they pass information upward. So, to play hardball, you must develop your own truth-telling network, or you will never be sure what the heart-of-the-matter issues really are. Truth-telling networks are very personal and largely informal, and may include colleagues, customers, advisors, friends, and family members.

An organization that is unwilling or not ready to face the heart of the matter is one doomed to inaction. It will be like a sitting duck in comparison to competitors that are able to face the heart of the matter. So it is the job of the hardball leader to compel his organization to face the heart of the matter and then plunge them into it.

Once you've entered the heart of the matter, however, how do you concentrate your energy and keep it focused on the heart-of-the-matter issues? Hardball leaders do it by thinking of themselves as being in a perpetual turnaround. Even if the company is already successful, or becomes so, they continue to try to make it better, to find new sources of competitive advantage, build a virtuous competitive cycle, answer new threats, serve new markets, or solve whatever new challenges arise.

Further, hardball leaders make the turnaround the mission of the entire management team. These leaders get their team to focus relentlessly on the objectives of the turnaround so that all their decisions are made and activities carried out within that context.

But it can be difficult for a management team to determine those objectives because their management agenda is already so full and the list of issues that seem to require attention is so long. Managers are asked to deal with a wide range of human resource issues, from development to empowerment; they are expected to manage relationships with customers and partners; they must think about the systems and processes of the enterprise; they want to keep abreast of developments in the industry and in the economy.

But, for most enterprises, these issues are rarely at the heart of the matter. They may seem important, but they are not crucial. Paying attention to them may distract management from the very small set of objectives that will make the largest difference in performance and will contribute the most to the turnaround. In fact, the objectives are likely to be one of the following:

- Rationalization of the portfolio of business activities
- De-averaging costs and prices
- Focusing products, services, and customers
- Turning the strengths of key competitors into weaknesses

A management team in turnaround mode cannot allow themselves to be distracted from these central objectives. Their people, intending to help in the turnaround, will propose new ideas in a constant stream. But new initiatives for change and improvement must be considered carefully and accepted only if they will further these objectives. To help them decide which initiatives to pursue, hardball leaders follow these guidelines:

- *Survive first, then gain competitive advantage.* The central message of this book is that sustained, profitable, and rewarding growth can only be achieved by gaining competitive advantage. But a company must have money to make the investments that lead to competitive advantage. So, the sources of cash must be identified and maximized. The consumers of cash must be minimized. All surplus cash must be focused first on survival and then, as soon as possible, on creating and building competitive advantage.

- *Make all efforts fast, focused, and fundamental.* Every project undertaken in a turnaround should deliver payback—demonstrable and quantifiable—in twelve to eighteen months. This is *fast.* Every chosen performance improvement project should be protected from the onslaught of "neighbor" projects that always move in next door and claim to be related. These projects must be banned. This is *focus.* And, as we've said, only those efforts that go to the heart of the matter should be considered and pursued. This is *fundamental.*

- *Don't allow people to identify obstacles to change without also proposing solutions to overcome them.* Naysayers, alarmists, and complainers are a drag on the progress of a turnaround; sometimes they can be its death. You want people to articulate problems and identify obstacles, but not without suggesting at least one way, preferably several ways, to solve the problem or bypass the obstacle.

- *Say yes or no but never maybe.* The greatest stress on any organization is the lack of clear direction. When a new initiative is proposed, leaders will often avoid making a yes or no decision on whether to proceed, giving the champion hope and allowing valuable time and resources to be consumed in planning or running a pilot. Similarly, leaders will often fail to make a yes or no decision on whether to continue a current initiative. They will let it keep going in the hope that it may eventually generate something positive. Or they may simply wish to avoid conflict with the champions of these efforts. Not good. Say yes or no but never maybe. Even if the answer is no, that need not mean the initiative is dead forever. New or better information may emerge that will allow the issue to be revisited. In the meantime, scarce recourses can be devoted completely to the items on the "fast, focused, and fundamental" agenda.

- *Communicate continuously and repeatedly with key people—employees, customers, suppliers, financiers.* The CEO of a successful turnaround told us that it was only when he had become thoroughly sick and tired of talking to key stakeholders about the turnaround that they really began to understand it and get behind it. People need to hear the logic for what is happening many more times than may seem reasonable to senior management. A good test of whether the message is getting through and taking hold: ask a third or fourth level employee what they think the company's strategy is.

- *Don't tolerate failure to deliver more than once.* A great threat to a turnaround comes from people who fail to deliver anything but excuses. Many a turnaround has been slowed or derailed because a key player fails to deliver, not just once, but two or three times. Hardball leaders in a turnaround have low tolerance for failure. Time is too precious. One failure may be understandable, even unavoidable. Two or three failures to deliver suggests a lack of will, incompetence, or even subversion. This expectation for successful execution must be stated and made painfully clear to everybody at the beginning of the turnaround effort; they should understand that there may well be casualties. People who don't deliver need to be counselled, cautioned, moved, or fired. Colonel John Boyd, head of the U.S. Air Force Weapons School for many years, is famous for criticizing his top officers in Europe for their low casualty rate during training. He believed it indicated that the pilots were not being pushed hard enough.

There are many ways to win at hardball, and every winner has his own style of play. We hope that you will take from this hardball playbook whatever you can to better your own game. We wish you success as you work to create competitive advantage, shake up your industry, strengthen the economy, and make the business world a place where the game is played hard but true.

NOTES

Chapter One: The Hardball Manifesto

1. The Boston Consulting Group, *Failure to Compete* (Boston: The Boston Consulting Group, 1973).

2. Brian Bremner and Chester Dawson, "Can Anything Stop Toyota?" *Business-Week*, 17 November 2003. Steve Lohr, "Is Wal-Mart Good for America?" *New York Times*, 7 December 2003, section 4, page 1. Adam Lashinsky, "Dell: Meanest Kid on the Block" *Fortune* web site, 15 September 2003, <http://www.fortune.com/fortune/bottomline/0,15704,486908,00.html>.

3. B. H. Liddell Hart, *Strategy*, 2d rev. ed. (New York: Signet, 1967), 145.

4. Southwest Airlines, *Southwest Airlines Co. 1993 Annual Report*, Dallas, 1993.

Chapter Two: Unleash Massive and Overwhelming Force

1. The GM story is composed from BCG analysis and sources in the public domain.

2. BCG analysis.

3. Danny Hakim, "Vehicle Sales for October Were Highest Ever in U.S." *New York Times*, 2 November 2001, C2.

4. Sholnn Freeman, "Auto Makers' 0% Financing Plans Spark Sales and Analyst Concern," *Wall Street Journal*, 30 October 2001, B10.

5. BCG analysis.

6. Steve Finlay, "Wagoner: 'Quit Whining,'" *Ward's Dealer Business*, 1 March 2003, 5.

7. The Frito-Lay story is based on Rob Lachenauer's experience working as a Frito-Lay employee from 1983 to 1986; interviews with several past and present Frito-Lay managers; Roger Enrico, telephone interview by authors, 23 March 2004; and public sources.

8. Steve Englander, e-mail to Rob Lachenauer, 1 August 2003.

Chapter Three: Exploit Anomalies

1. Joe Girard with Stanley H. Brown, *How to $ell Anything to Anybody* (New York: Warner Books, 1977), 47–50.

2. Ibid., 47–50.

3. The Wausau Papers story is based on experience and analysis gained from BCG engagements with the company. The story is told fully in Michael J. Kronenwetter, *A Century of Wausau Paper* (Wausau: Marathon Communications, 1999).

Chapter Four: Threaten Your Competitor's Profit Sanctuaries

1. The VacuCorp and SweepCo story is based on a real case, but has been fictionalized.

Chapter Five: Take It and Make It Your Own

1. Bill Saporito, "What Sam Walton Taught America," *Fortune*, 4 May 1992, 66–67.

2. The Batesville story is based on experience and analysis gained from a BCG engagement with Batesville.

3. The Ford story is based on experience and analysis gained from BCG engagements in the auto industry. Quotes from players in the story are paraphrased.

4. The Ryanair story is based on analysis and experience gained from a BCG engagements in the airline industry, as well as public sources.

Chapter Six: Entice Your Competitor into Retreat

1. The Federal-Mogul and JPI story is based on analysis and experience gained from a BCG engagement with Federal-Mogul, and public sources.

2. *Magnum Force,* motion picture, directed by Ted Post (Burbank, CA: Warner Brothers, 1973).

Chapter Seven: Break Compromises

1. The CarMax story is based on Austin Ligon, telephone interview by authors, 25 November 2003, and BCG analysis of information from public sources.

2. Kathleen Kerwin, "The Shape of a New Machine," *BusinessWeek*, 24 July 1995, 60.

Chapter Eight: Hardball M&A

1. Richard A. Knox, "Hospitals Expect Merger to Save Millions: MGH, Brigham Super-Hospital Deal Would Change Face of Boston Medical Establishment," *Boston Globe,* 9 December 1993, 1.

2. Richard A. Knox, "Harvard Dean Seeks to Unite Hospitals, Fears Split of Medical School's Research, Teaching Programs," *Boston Globe,* 30 October 1997, C1.

3. The Cisco story is based on analysis of information from public sources.

4. The Newell story is based on information from public sources and interviews with Newell executives.

5. Bob Papoe, "Merger Creates Largest Doormaker," *Toronto Star,* 28 October 1989, C1.

6. Cherilyn Radbourne, "Masonite International Corp.: Can't Knock It," *RBC Capital Markets,* 11 August 2003, 14.

7. "Philip Orsino, "Opportunity Knocked," *National Post,* 1 November 2003, 34.

Chapter Nine: Changes in the Field of Play

1. This material is based on the book by BCG colleagues Michael J. Silverstein and Neil Fiske, with John Butman, *Trading Up: The New American Luxury* (New York: Portfolio, 2003).

2. Nanette Byrnes, "Is Wilbur Ross Crazy?," *BusinessWeek,* 22 December 2003, 74.

3. Anthony Bianco and Wendy Zeller, "Is Wal-Mart Too Powerful?" *Business-Week,* 6 October 2003, 100.

4. Steve Lohr, "Is Wal-Mart Good for America?" *New York Times,* 7 December 2003. section 4, page 1.

ACKNOWLEDGMENTS

In creating this book, we have been helped by many clients, colleagues, and partners.

Our most important acknowledgment goes to our life partners, C. Henri and Catherine, whose unwavering support was the *sine qua non* of this endeavor.

The book would not exist without the inspiration of the hardball leadership of dozens of businesspeople. We particularly want to thank Steve Englander, Roger Enrico, Dennis Gormley, Michael Jordan, Bill Klehm, Brock Leach, Austin Ligon, Dean John McArthur, Jeri Opera, Steve Reinemund, Charlie Rogers, Lonnie Smith, and Pat Ward.

Many of our colleagues at The Boston Consulting Group shared their knowledge, assisted our efforts, and provided comment on drafts. Thanks to James Abraham, Stephen Amery, Hans-Paul Buerkner, John Clarkeson, Tom Corra, Paul Cort, Amy Davy, Mike Deimler, Grant Freeland, Karen Gordon, Stuart Grief, Gerry Hansell, Kris Holland, Matt Holland, Barry Jones, Tom King, Bill Matassoni, Dave Matheson, K. C. Munuz, David Pecaut, Lon Povich, Stefan Rasch, Bronwyn Romain, Michael Shanahan, Larry Shulman, Michael Silverstein, Miki Tsusaka, Mary Wilson-Smith, and David Young. Special thanks to Carl Stern for his counsel and comment.

We also benefited from the insight and comment of many readers outside of BCG, including Marv Adams, John Browett, Dan Carp, George Derhofer, Tom Erixon, Alan Feldman, Bruce Harreld, Jeff Immelt, Egore G. Klats, Jeff Kuster, Catherine Lachenauer, Delia Lachenauer, Steve Lohr, Mackey McDonald, Allan Ramsey, Paul Ritvo, Fred Smith, and Henri Lee Stalk.

Finally, we thank our research, writing, and publishing team, including our editor at Harvard Business School Press, Melinda Merino, and our contributing editors, Eric Calonius, Paul Hemp, Steve Prokesch, and Tom Stewart. Special thanks to our collaborating editor, John Butman, for his many efforts in bringing the book to fruition.

INDEX

ABOUT THE AUTHORS

George Stalk joined The Boston Consulting Group (BCG) in 1978 and is now a senior vice president based in Toronto. He has also worked in the Boston, Chicago, and Tokyo offices. Stalk focuses on international strategy and time-based competition, advising clients in retailing, automotive, and other industries. He is the coauthor (with Thomas H. Hout) of *Competing Against Time* and (with James C. Abegglen) of *Kaisha: The Japanese Corporation.* His *Harvard Business Review* article "Time—The Next Source of Competitive Advantage" won the McKinsey Award in 1988. Stalk holds a B.S. in engineering mechanics from the University of Michigan, an M.S. in aeronautics and astronautics from Massachusetts Institute of Technology, and an M.B.A. from Harvard Business School. Before joining BCG, he held positions with Applicon, Inc. and Exxon Research and Engineering.

Rob Lachenauer is CEO of GEO$_2$, a company whose mission is to reduce harmful emissions from cars, trucks, and other products that use internal combustion engines. Lachenauer was formerly a vice president with BCG, specializing in the automotive industry, consumer retailing, and branding. He is the author of several BCG publications on creating and managing brand value. Prior to joining BCG, Lachenauer held sales and marketing positions at Frito-Lay. He earned a B.A. in English from Cornell University and an M.B.A. from Harvard Business School.

John Butman is the author, editor, or collaborating writer of more than a dozen books, primarily on the subjects of business management and social change. His titles include *Trading Up: The New American Luxury; Real Boys: Rescuing Our Sons from the Myths of Boyhood;* and *Townie,* a novel.